Tribute to Wilkie

THE EXHIBITION HAS BEEN SPONSORED BY
THE DISTILLERS COMPANY PLC

Tribute to Wilkie

from the National Gallery of Scotland
with contributions by Turner,
Landseer, Frith and
others

LINDSAY ERRINGTON

The National Galleries of Scotland

Copyright © 1985
The Trustees of the
National Galleries of Scotland

ISBN 0 903148 60 9

Designed by George Mackie RDI
Typeset by Speedspools, Edinburgh
Printed by Alna Press Ltd, Broxburn, West Lothian

Contents

LENDERS TO THE EXHIBITION

PHOTOGRAPHIC CREDITS

Photographs from the Royal Collection are reproduced by gracious
permission of Her Majesty the Queen. All other photographs were
supplied by the owners, with the following exceptions: figs. 2, 8, 20,
22, 23, 24, 26, 29, 32, 42, 53 from negatives held by the S.N.P.G.

The following line illustrations at the heads or tail of the chapters
are details from Wilkie drawings in the collection of the National
Gallery of Scotland. Page 1, D2300A; p.26, D3941; p.70, D3924;
p.93, D4986. The drawing of Cults Manse on p.6 is a detail from a
drawing in the Paul Mellon Collection, Yale Center for British
Art, Newhaven, USA. The drawing of figures on p.53 is a study for
Chelsea Pensioners reproduced by courtesy of Christie's. The line
engraving on p.95 is a detail from *Les politiques de village* after
Wilkie's *Village Politicians* published in Duchesne, *Museum of
Painting and Sculpture,* vol. xv, London 1834, p.1020. The colour
transparency of Frith's *Railway Station* was supplied by the
Bridgeman Art Library.

Foreword

WILKIE was born in Fife on 18 November 1785. The two hundred years since his birth saw first, his meteoric transformation from complete obscurity as a poverty-stricken Scots countryboy newly arrived in London, into a brilliant artist of European celebrity working for statesmen and kings, and then sadly, a decline into semi-obscurity again. His *Chelsea Pensioners* of 1822 was the first painting for which a barrier was ever erected at the Royal Academy to prevent the crowds crushing it in their excitement. For it the Duke of Wellington paid the artist a record price. Rival monarchs, George IV and the King of Bavaria, contended for the possession of another Wilkie, *Reading the Will*. Now perhaps, alas, he is better known through Turner's painting of his funeral, *Peace, Burial at Sea*, than through any work of his own. The last major Wilkie exhibition was held in Edinburgh and London in 1958, and though it may have gained him many individual admirers it did not, in the long term, go far towards restoring him to a significant position in the history of British painting.

In celebrating his bi-centenary this Gallery decided therefore to avoid a repetition of the 1958 exhibition, and try instead to demonstrate the crucial role Wilkie's art played in the development of Victorian genre painting. Without Wilkie the paintings of Mulready, Landseer, Frith, and even Holman Hunt, would hardly be as we see them today.

The National Gallery is particularly grateful to Her Majesty The Queen for graciously lending Wilkie's *Penny Wedding* and Bird's *Country Choristers*; and to all other lenders, named and anonymous, whose willingness to give up their pictures for the time has made this exhibition possible. We would, in addition, like to extend thanks for various kinds of information and help to William G.F.Boag, Patricia Campbell, Louisa Coddrington, Hugh Cheape, Judy Egerton, Clare Meredith, Hamish Miles, Richard Ormond, William Payne, John Pinkerton, Marcia Pointon, Sara Stevenson, Meta Viles, and Christopher Wood.

We are also extremely grateful to the Distillers Company PLC for their very generous sponsorship; and to Dr Lindsay Errington for her scholarship and enthusiasm in the preparation of the exhibition.

Timothy Clifford, *Director*

Introduction : the Reputation of Wilkie

THE THREE greatest British artists of the first three decades of the nineteenth century were two landscapists and a figure painter, Constable, Turner, and Wilkie. Wilkie's national—and international— reputation was in his own lifetime as high or higher than that of the other two men. Constable was his personal friend, Turner something between a keen rival and a distant acquaintance (he did not come to Wilkie's house until 1821), but a rival whose *Peace Burial at Sea* is a most moving obituary and tribute from one great painter to another. Nevertheless by means of one of those curious fictitious querks which are passed off and accepted as genuine historical fact, it has recently been unquestioningly assumed that all the most important British painting of the earlier nineteenth century was devoted to landscape whilst significant developments in figurative art did not really occur before the Pre-Raphaelites—two decades ago one might have said 'before Whistler'. In a huge recent study of the *Art of the nineteenth century* (Rosenblum and Janson, London 1984), Wilkie's masterpiece, *The Chelsea Pensioners reading the Gazette of the Battle of Waterloo* (*cat.38*), a landmark in British art, is mentioned only because Géricault made some favourable comments on it. Géricault's biographer Eitner even finds it necessary to explain away these comments as if the taking of them at face value would in some manner diminish the hero's stature as an artist. He has been caught in the act of betraying a seeming bad taste, but we must understand that of course he did not *really* admire Wilkie.[1]

If on the other hand, we return to the year 1853, when Victorian painting was moving into a phase of exuberant creative energy, we find that the critic Tom Taylor had this to say, 'The class of pictures which now employs the largest number of artists, and is most sought after and best paid, combining some of the qualities of historical painting with still life—what is called *genre*-painting—may almost be said to have been founded by Wilkie, . . . this style affords a loophole through which to escape from the sole dominion of the portrait-painter, in a time when the public functions of Art are still little appreciated. In works of this kind may be exhibited the highest qualities of invention and expression.'[2] In other words Wilkie was the salvation of imaginative figurative art in Britain, by his creation of a viable alternative to the huge and bombastic history paintings which no one had any real use for.

Wilkie was the creator of what we now call Victorian genre. In this perhaps lies the secret of his present non-existent reputation. The hagiography of Turner is traceable back to the efforts of Ruskin and it was the intricate pattern of nature discovered in the form of rocks, trees and clouds which stimulated Ruskin's own creative imagination, not the intricate patterns of human motive and behaviour. 'Much disappointed with Wilkie's life: he is a thoroughly low person and his biographer worse' was Ruskin's crisp youthful dismissal in 1843. But Ruskin, one might object, did not care for Constable's work either, and Constable's reputation has survived intact. Indeed, art lovers who took the trouble to look for themselves have found it easy to discard Ruskin's view of Wilkie. 'Dr Honeyman confessed that he had been for many years misled by the views of certain critics from Ruskin onwards concerning Sir David Wilkie's contribution to British art . . . His brilliant career in London and his phenomenal success in academic and Court circles made fascinating reading, and the range of his achievement (illustrated by numerous lantern slides) was clearly demonstrated.' Dr Honeyman, the Director of Glasgow City Art Galleries, made his confession in a public lecture of 1940, and it was duly reported in *The Glasgow Herald*. Although he did not name those critics after Ruskin whose adverse opinions had also affected appreciation of Wilkie, it is possible I believe, from our own standpoint at the end of this century, to see how extraordinarily damaging to the understanding of Wilkie was Roger Fry's defence of the modern movements in art which had sprung from Cézanne.

Fry's appreciation of Wilkie was limited to those aspects which can also be found in Cézanne—'sensitiveness of line', 'plenitude of form', figures 'solidly constructed' and a 'fine sense of placing'.[3] Wilkie did truly possess these important qualities, and so too have many other artists, but it is not in these that the essential qualities of his unique pictorial gift are shown, and what was most valuable about his art was unfortunately something Fry could not acknowledge as art at all. Like Taylor, Fry saw that Wilkie had founded Victorian genre painting, but to Fry this was a crime. 'Finally the story-telling aspect of the picture tends to become too

1. Formal significance in peasants by Cézanne. *The Card Players*

2. Psychological significance in peasants by Wilkie.
   Detail from *Village Politicians* (cat.20)

3. Social significance in peasants by Israels. Detail from *The frugal meal*

prominent . . . his desire to make the point of his anecdote is too evident and leads him to sacrifice too much to it. In this respect perhaps Wilkie is more responsible than any one for much future disaster to our art . . . he gradually put more and more weight on the anecdote and less and less on his design, so that he helped to start British art on that facile descent to Avernus . . . But in some of his designs we have nothing to complain of, the story interferes no more with the design than it does in Ostade.' A comparison between Cézanne's *Card Players* which Fry admired enormously, and the central group from Wilkie's *Village Politicians* (*cat.20*) perhaps makes Fry's point more fully than words can do. His idea of 'significant form' as exemplified by the Cézanne was in all respects the opposite of the significant form exemplified by Wilkie. In Wilkie's work all forms, inanimate objects, furniture, clothing, heads, hands and the entire human body are 'significant' as they are to us in everyday life, for we comprehend the tastes, preferences, past history and momentary present thoughts of other people as much by looking at them as listening to them. At the same moment as we perceive, we recognise and interpret. Fry wanted, in looking at painting, to divorce these processes, and he assumed—what is very questionable—that it is possible to see form without interpreting it, to see a face or body just as abstract geometrical solids. The force of Wilkie's desire to see people as people, with wishes, memories, feelings and relationships to other people intrudes itself willy nilly upon any desire to relegate them in Cézanne's phrase to 'cylinders, cones and cubes'. What in Wilkie was not line, void or solid was to Fry an anecdote, and anecdotes as we all know, are the writer's province. It was left to Sickert, the brilliant and provocative attacker of Fry's views—and an artist of far greater stature— to defend the art of narrative and psychology that derived from Wilkie.

(4)

Fry's significant form carries less weight with us now, but unfortunately for Wilkie recent art critics have required a new kind of significance from the pictorial artist, political significance, contemporary relevance, an art of commitment dedicated to social reform. To these critics exploited women, fallen women, starved sempstresses, squalid working classes, evicted Irish, suicides, mad-houses, Géricault's *Raft of the Medusa*, Manet's *Execution of the Emperor Maximilian* are significant, *Village Festivals, Penny Weddings* and *Chelsea Pensioners* are not. Yet a critic of 1860 wrote of Wilkie that 'he led the minds of the richer classes to sympathise with the joys and sorrows of their poorer brethren and thus elevated himself to the high position of a right-minded philanthropist. What Cowper and Crabbe were among poets, Wilkie was among painters: his pictures are didactic poems'.[4] The Directors of the British Institution hid Wilkie's *Distraining for Rent* (cat.37) in a dark lumber room because they believed it was a seditious attack upon landed proprietors, and the writer Washington Irving who, with the artist Leslie, contrived to find it in this hiding place, looked at it for a long time in silence until Leslie, glancing at him, saw that his eyes were filled with tears.[5]

Two hundred years have passed since Wilkie's birth in 1785, and it is more than time to look at him again and see what he does have to offer of his own, instead of expunging his name from its deserved place in the record of art history because he has failed to comply with some theory of art not yet invented when he was at work. Although Fry believed that Wilkie perhaps 'had no very marked personal vision' it is only an artist of the most exceptional original vision who can influence his contemporaries and successors to the extent that Wilkie did. This bi-centenary exhibition together with the essays in this book are an attempt to demonstrate the nature and originality of Wilkie's vision by tracing its effects upon the work of British artists. By seeing the fragmented reflections of so many of Wilkie's ideas and methods appearing and re-appearing in rather different paintings by other people we can perhaps then return to Wilkie himself with an enlarged and more truthful image of his own achievement.

Not every British artist who fell under Wilkie's spell is featured here, and no foreign artists at all. He did nonetheless influence painters in France, Germany, Russia and the United States, some of them artists who had never seen a single original specimen of his work, but had only come across one or two of the prints after his *Blind Fiddler* (cat.19) or *Village Politicians*—but this is perhaps a subject for another exhibition, a wider ranging exhibition than the present one, comprehending artists as diverse as Delacroix, Fedotov and Eastman Jackson.

NOTES : INTRODUCTION

1. L. E. A. Eitner, *Géricault, his life and work* London 1983, pp.218-19.

2. Tom Taylor, *Life of Benjamin Robert Haydon* in 3 vols, 2nd edition, London 1853, Vol.3, pp.358-9.

3. Roger Fry, *Wilkie*, in *Reflections on British Painting* London 1934, pp.96-99.

4. *The Art Journal* 1860, p.108.

5. *Autobiographical recollections of Charles Robert Leslie* ed. Tom Taylor, 2 vols, London 1860, vol.1, p.215.

Folklore and the Vernacular Tradition

WILKIE was born in the Manse of Cults in Fife on 18 November 1785. After his artistic training at the Trustees' Academy, and before he moved to London in 1805, he lived at home painting portraits, mainly of local landowners and their families. He had already painted various small genre scenes in the tradition of Carse and Allan, but his first really important imaginative composition was his *Pitlessie Fair* (*cat.2*), a portrait of his own village, carried out for Kinnear of Kinloch, an estate a few miles north from Pitlessie.

An eighteenth-century interpretation of the aims of the Dutch masters whom Wilkie followed for *Pitlessie Fair* was provided by Joshua Reynolds in his *Discourses,* which Wilkie is known to have read. 'A history-piece is properly a portrait of themselves, whether they describe the inside or outside of their houses, we have their own people engaged in their own peculiar occupations; working or drinking, playing or fighting . . . they exhibit all the minute particularities of a nation differing in several respects from the rest of mankind.' This ethnographic explanation of Dutch art, though it has recently been superseded by other types of interpretation, can still stand as a very fair description, not only of what Wilkie in 1804 must have supposed the Dutch painters meant to do, but also of what he meant to do himself. *Pitlessie Fair* has of course its parents in Scots vernacular poems or ballads describing fairs, as well as in the eighteenth-century drawings of Scottish fairs or racecourses by David Allan and Alexander Carse, but it possesses an extreme factual precision as to persons and locality, a scrupulous fidelity in the information provided, by which it surpasses and differs from its predecessors. Wilkie's care for factual accuracy is apparent in the inscriptions which record, on his preparatory drawing, the material substances of which the various roofs and walls are composed, and we know that he was equally accurate about the

4. *Pitlessie Fair* by Wilkie (*cat.2*)

fairgoers themselves, snatching their features by stealth as they listened to his father preaching in Cults Church.

The Church and manse of Cults where the Wilkie family lived, stand about a mile outside the village of Pitlessie. The village was part of the parish of Cults, but the inhabitants of the manse were not really part of the village. Besides this physical detachment there must have been a social detachment as well. The *New Statistical Account of Cults Parish*, published in 1838 describes the painting of *Pitlessie Fair* as containing 'portraits of Wilkie himself, his father, brothers and sisters, and of many other characters known in the parish and neighbourhood'. These family portraits were not specially identified by the writer, but it was scarcely necessary for him to do so. As one looks at the painting, certain figures emerge as better dressed, and dressed in a rather different style from the others. The gentlemen wear smart hats and well cut coats which fit nicely round the shoulders. The countrymen, by contrast, are wearing bonnets, or slightly battered hats, and loose, crumpled, coarsely cut coats. The country-women's heads are covered with floppy linen mutches or caps. The female Wilkies wear neat stiff bonnets or small, fashionable caps. Wilkie's father is probably the figure in profile, with a cane below his arm and a crisp white cravat, who stands immediately above the old man patting the little boy on the head. Wilkie's mother and sister Helen are almost certainly the two ladies with their backs to us who hold the arms of the painter himself or his brother, at the tented stall in the very centre of the picture. Next in degree come the well dressed farmers and their wives whose children are

5. Smartly dressed members of the Wilkie family
   at a stall in *Pitlessie Fair* (*cat.2* detail)

6. Small but 'improved' cattle, and an antiquated
   chimney in Wilkie's *Pitlessie Fair* (*cat.2* detail)

equipped with hats, stockings and shoes, clean collars and pinafores, and
lastly the barefooted highland drover's boy with torn breeks, and the
hatless, shoeless, ragged child being patted on the head. Adults and
children, there are over a hundred figures present, out of a parish that
according to the 1801 Government census consisted of 699 inhabitants.

The fair itself was an annual event held for the sale of agricultural
stock, mainly cattle, which took place 'the second tuesday of May, old

style'. It was selected by Wilkie as the most appropriate occasion for assembling a complete representation of the parish at all social levels. The only other equally representative occasion would have been sermon-time in his father's church, and this, the painter wisely discarded as an idea. Considering his status as Minister's son it would have undoubtedly led to problems and local hostility.

It is perhaps worth asking why Wilkie wished to reconstruct this record of his parish in paint. Apart from the obvious reply that he believed this was what the seventeenth-century Dutch artists had done, there may well have been a second contributory factor. In 1790, when the artist was five years old, Sir John Sinclair circulated what he called 'a variety of queries' amongst the Clergy of the Church of Scotland in order to elucidate 'the Natural History and Political State of that Country'. He had in mind a record, like that of the Doomsday Book, covering the whole of Scotland. The units of his record were the accounts of the individual parishes based on the returns of the local clergy and the whole record was published volume by volume between the years 1791 and 1799 under the title of *The First Statistical Account of Scotland.* The state of the nation as a whole is thus established by a process of addition. The state of each parish is regarded as the critical thing. In a sense the parish *is* the nation in little. Wilkie's father's account of Cults parish and Pitlessie Village was published in 1791 when the painter was six, and the occasion was marked forever in the child's memory by the fact that Sinclair sent an engraving of a soldier to all the clergy who had participated. This engraving was the first picture Wilkie ever copied.[1] The Reverend David Wilkie provided an account of such matters as the number of inhabitants, their education, occupations, wages, fuel, the progress of agriculture, number of ale houses and the worth of the living including the glebe. It is a terse but in its own way a very complete description, and the son's painting of Pitlessie is perhaps most truly understood if one regards it as the visual analogue to his father's written portrait. Like the statistical account itself it provides information on Pitlessie at a given moment in time, on which the historian can rely, but it is different information. We are so much in the habit of regarding paintings as works of the imagination only, and *The Statistical Account* as a source for factual information only, that we miss an obvious truth. Both are efforts of the imagination to win a comprehensive picture of the facts, and both are equally conditioned by their common historical period.

Wilkie's picture can not only supply information concerning matters of detail not mentioned in the *Account,* it can also draw attention to what was physically absent from the village. The non-existence of all rones (gutters), downpipes, and chimney pots are structural features which the modern home owner notices at once, though naturally Wilkie's father does not allude to them.[2] Further peculiarities are the use of sods of turf as a protection along the ridges of the roofs where today we would expect ridge tiles or metal flashings, the curious wooden structure balanced on the

7. Drawing of a cattle market by Geikie produced 1821-2 after seeing
Pitlessie exhibited in Edinburgh

gable end of the ruined house on the right, and considerable diversity both
in building materials themselves and in their use. The village contains
single and two storied houses, windows and chimneys of various patterns,
including buildings with no apparent chimneys at all, roofs of thatch, tile,
and turf, wall or chimney surfaces comprising wood, brick, stone and a
brownish harled finish. Some of the buildings are detached, others form
gently undulating rows that follow the undulations of the ground and the
bend of the concealed burn. Wilkie was particularly careful to note the
building materials on his preparatory drawing which lists in a numbered
key '1. Harld wall/2. Whinstone do. [i.e. ditto]/3. tile roof/4. thack roof/5.
old do./6. brick'. The Pitlessie he presents to us is thus not a hazily
traditional 'vernacular' village of no special date, but a village precisely
trapped in a period of transition between old and modern building
methods.

Architecturally the period was one of steady up-grading and improvement, which the cottages exhibit in a greater or lesser degree. The ruined
building on the far right belongs to a pattern of construction becoming
obsolete, with its crudely shaped roof timbers and disintegrating wicker
chimney that, in its better days would have been bound round and
anchored in place with ropes of straw. The remnant of the internal part of
this chimney structure can still be seen hanging down the wall beside the

8. *Skirling Fair* by James Howe. This portrait of Skirling village near
Biggar c.1830 echoes Wilkie's *Pitlessie* (cat.7)

heads of the horses occupying it as a makeshift stable. As with the buildings so with the livestock—and here the picture corrects or amplifies the
written *Account*. Who would suppose, looking at Wilkie's puny cows and
undersized horses, that they had been the subjects of a deliberate policy of
improvement in the parish, by better feeding and breeding, for the last
twenty or thirty years? Yet such was indeed the case, so that what to our
eyes appear substandard cows, to the eyes of Wilkie's friends were very
adequate cows, of which the farmer could even be proud. It is most certainly not an illegitimate use of the painting to harvest such un-aesthetic
information from it, because only Wilkie's own care to record these facts
now enables us to receive them.

In the same year that Wilkie painted *Pitlessie Fair* was born, in the
same County of Fife, the elder of the two brothers Bethune, poverty-
stricken rural labourers who are now remembered for writing their *Tales
of the Scottish Peasantry*. Their description of the fictitious Fife village,
Nethertown draws attention to the modernising process that we see at
work on the homes in Pitlessie. The farm at Nethertown was modern, with
a slated roof, 'but in the appearance of the other houses, all the rustic
simplicity and rude architecture of an earlier age may still be traced. After
all the innovations and improvements to which the first thirty years of the
nineteenth century gave birth, there they stood with their low walls, built
in some instances with clay instead of mortar—roofs composed of alternate
layers of thatch and turf—chimney-tops with a rope of twisted straw
around them to keep them together, and doors so low that their inhabi-

tants were obliged to loot low before they could enter . . . The houses were disposed in no regular order, but stood in groups of two or three together, generally in the lowest places of an undulating surface'.[3] Of another, similar village, in another of their stories, the Bethunes wrote 'and such as it was it never can be again'. Both they, and Wilkie seem bent on describing the old villages partly out of a desire to record what was passing away, and this is an aspect of Wilkie's work to which we shall have to return.

If one looks at the very centre of *Pitlessie Fair,* the brightly coloured group of drummer and recruiting sergeant chatting up a young country man, remind the viewer of the contemporary war with France. After the peace of Amiens (1802) Britain reduced its army so drastically that when war was declared again in 1803, frenzied efforts at recruitment were necessary to restore the forces to a viable strength. The military frenzy is even reflected in the small boy squabbling with his sister for the possession of a toy soldier. The uniform of Wilkie's recruiting party presents certain oddities such as cockades on the wrong side, but it does seem as though we are seeing soldiers of the regular army and not militia men or volunteers. Neither the militia nor the volunteers recruited in this manner, and the Pitlessie volunteers had, in any case, been disbanded two years earlier in 1802. We are apparently looking at a Scottish lowland foot regiment, just possibly the Cameronians, the only non-highland regiment with yellow facings. The drummerboy, who always formed part of a recruiting party and might be as young as eleven, wears the same colours, red and yellow, but reversed to make him conspicuous. The piper does not indicate a highland regiment. Pipers were present, but only unofficially, in the army at this date, and often appeared on the role as drummers. The two figures with the piper and drummer cannot be identified as to rank, though their hair worn in queues indicates that they are not officers. The figure in brown who aims a blow with his stick at passing cattle is the chief puzzle. There were no brown regular army uniforms at this date, but he may perhaps be accompanying the recruiting party on behalf of the town.[4] The total effect is of something observed by Wilkie not something invented.

The change from an older building style to a modern one, and the improved cattle thus locate the portrait of Pitlessie in time, a time of change and modernisation, whilst the recruitment scene pinpoints the moment more exactly as being the fair of the year that followed the redeclaration of war with France. These factors are counterweights in the painting to all those aspects that suggest to the modern viewer immemorial rural tradition and regular annual recurrence. Tradition and modernity, custom and change, the perpetual and the momentary, are thus balanced in the portrait of *Pitlessie Fair.* In the work of Wilkie's followers emphasis was to fall increasingly on memory and tradition at the expense of the present moment.

In *Pitlessie* the Scottishness of the subject is only latent or implicit. Since Wilkie had never yet been out of his own country he could not select for special emphasis any of the peculiar features distinguishing Scottish

9. A cross-section of rural Scottish society at play in Harvey's sketch for the *Curlers* (*cat.10*)

from, say, English fairs. He had the picture in London with him during his first years there and it was included in his London one man show of 1812. It was not engraved, and not surprisingly made far more impact on Scottish art than on art south of the border. Walter Geikie who must have seen *Pitlessie* when it was at the R.I. in 1821, was transformed by the sight from a painter of stiffly upright detached wooden figures, spaced evenly out in rows, into a painter of animated figure groups and clusters. Wilkie's picture not only gave him confidence in his chosen genre, but showed him the value of psychological observation and group interaction. Since Geikie was a deaf mute, forced to rely on his eyes for comprehension of any situation, Wilkie's treatment must have come to him like a revelation. In subsequent pictures he followed the Wilkie method of figure relationships and, without departing from it, enriched it with endless new and original observations of his own.

Harvey probably saw *Pitlessie* at the same R.I. exhibition. Its overall canvas shape, and chain effect of strikingly varied figure groups seem to be the main influence behind his *Curlers* (*cat.10*). The subject too—for curling is an intrinsically Scottish sport—suggests the idea that national, as well as individual characteristics may be revealed by the painter most successfully whilst the subject is at play. Since Harvey's picture embraces the whole spectrum of rural society, with laird and minister joining the other more lowly contestants, it shares something of *Pitlessie*'s social comprehensiveness.

Geikie was also receptive to the antiquarian or conservationist aspect of Wilkie's picture, and his oeuvre includes many drawings made probably in the Lothian area (one is identified as Cousland), of farm kitchens.[5] These are full of the kind of fireplace and window features that improvements were gradually phasing out. On the whole, however, especially as the century wore on, the finished paintings of Wilkie's followers tended to lay more emphasis on the nostalgia of the sentiment than the precision of the record. This is perhaps most obviously the case in the work of Phillip,

10. Phillip's *Scotch fair* includes a recruiting party, horses,
cattle, sidestalls, children and dogs in groupings that recall those
of *Pitlessie Fair* (*cat.9*)

whose *Scotch Fair* (*cat.9*) of 1849 owes much to *Pitlessie* in subject and
incident, though in style it relates to the Wilkie of a later date whose own
attitude towards his Scottish subjects was beginning to change.

It was not to be expected that Wilkie, after many years residence in
London should preserve so unselfconscious an approach to his country and
its culture. The scenery and the poetry of Burns, and poetry and novels of
Scott were turning Scotland into a tourist attraction. The Scottish artist in
London had many disadvantages to cope with, but one momentary advan-
tage he did have. He was at first the only purveyor, as far as painting went,
of that desirable new article, Scottish traditional culture, the real thing,
exported from the land of Burns, not to be confused with inferior imita-
tions. When, in 1817 Wilkie returned to Scotland on a visit to collect
ethnographical material for his *Penny Wedding* (*cat.3*), it was as a tourist
he went and almost as a foreigner that he appraised the situation. 'Scotland is most remarkable however as a volume of history. It is the land of
tradition & of poetry. every district has some scene in it of real or fictitious
events treasured with a sort of religious care in the minds of the
inhabitants.'[6]

When Wilkie was touring Scotland, on this visit, gathering picturesque material, he made the drawing of an interior at Perth (fig.11), one
of many such drawings that were to recur throughout his life. It shows a
kitchen, including the floor, ceiling timbers, a fireplace with an iron
swey for suspending a pot, a dresser a couple of stools, and various
utensils and tools laid about not to suit the picturesque fancy of an

11. A Perth kitchen recorded by Wilkie on his Scottish tour of 1817

artist but quite obviously just where the cottage inhabitants had last put them down. Anyone who has used the Country Life Archive in the National Museum of Antiquities of Scotland will be irresistably reminded by Wilkie's drawing of the archival photographs of rural Scottish interiors, and rightly, for these photographs are the true descendants of Wilkie's drawing. *The Rural Architecture of Scotland* (Fenton and Walker, Edinburgh 1981) which lists the survey bodies, archive and printed sources from which evidence concerning old rural building can be extracted, points out the great difficulty of dating still existing buildings or of dating changes within these buildings. Although photography was in use from the 1840s, interior photography, such as the authors employ to illustrate their chapter on the housing of farm workers, was scarcely feasible until the end of the nineteenth century. Thus drawings such as Wilkie made from 1817 are for most of the century the only satisfactory evidence—because far more specific than even the most detailed written account—of the interiors of rural cottages, describing not only what was inside these houses but exactly where it was. It seems entirely possible that in the drawings of Wilkie and his followers there is a resource that the social and architectural historians have scarcely begun to exploit or appreciate, but however true that may be, Wilkie's activities in this line can only be properly understood in relation to the Scottish conservation or revival movement in literature of the early nineteenth century.

A significant figure in the Scottish vernacular revival of the late eighteenth century, whom Wilkie had of course encountered at the

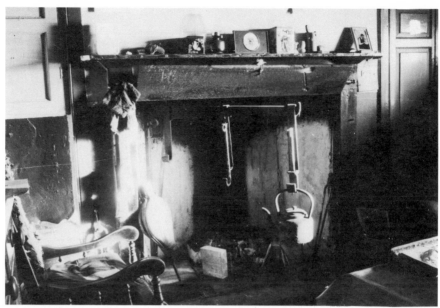

12. A Scottish kitchen by a twentieth-century photographer, in the National Museum of Antiquities, continues the Wilkie tradition of visual recording

Trustees' Academy when he was an art student, was the Board's Clerk, George Thomson. Thomson's clerkship was simply an administrative post. His fame rests not on this but on his passion for collecting old Scottish tunes and his friendship with the poet Burns who wrote or re-wrote the words for Thomson's collection of traditional Scottish melodies. Thomson commenced his project in 1792 and published the songs together with Burns' verses in six volumes between 1793 and 1841. *Duncan Gray* (the tune) was described by Burns to Thomson in December 1792 as 'that kind of light-horse gallop of an air which precludes sentiment'. In January of the next year Thomson acknowledged the receipt of the poem itself commenting 'Duncan is indeed a lad of grace, and his humour will endear him to everybody'.[7]

On 4 July 1807, Wilkie by now in London, and already celebrated as a Scottish artist of peasant life, was sent a letter by George Thomson requesting 'that you will paint me a picture in your best manner, either from *Duncan Gray* or *Muirland Willie*'.[8] Although Wilkie did not immediately respond to Thomson's first plea for a picture illustrating *Duncan Gray* he must have held the subject in reserve as a possibility, for in 1814 he completed his *Refusal from Burns' Song of Duncan Gray* and exhibited it as a companion to *The Letter of Introduction*. This was sold to a southern buyer, but in 1819 Wilkie painted a smaller replica with some variations of the *Duncan Gray* subject (*cat.22*) and sold it to George Thomson. It was engraved, and this led to a quarrel between the two men in 1822 when Thomson wished, against the artist's will, to print the engraving in his small octavo edition of the songs. Wilkie offered to buy the plate but his

13. Wilkie co-operates with the Scottish folksong collector George Thomson. An illustration to Burns' song *Duncan Gray* which had been published by Thomson (*cat.22*)

offer was refused, and by 1828 Thomson had sold the picture itself—apparently to pay a debt—although he had 'fondly hoped . . . (it) would have gladdened my eyes as long as I lived'.[9]

Thomson's alternative suggestion in the letter of 1807 was for an illustration to another of his Scottish songs, *Muirland Willie*. 'It is a merry making which you may represent in any manner you think most agreable and being within doors can receive a more beautiful effect of light and shadow and tone of colour, than day light compositions of figures. I know not whether the following stanza has attracted your notice, the last in Muirland Willy,

14. The legendary fiddler Niel Gow plays for eighteenth-century
Scottish country dancers in Wilkie's nostalgic *Penny Wedding*
of 1819 (*cat.3*)

> Sic hirdum dirdum and sic din,
> Sic laughing, quaffing, and sic fun,
> The Minstrels (the fiddlers) they did never blin'
> Wi' mickle mirth and glee
> And ay they bobbit and ay they beckt
> And ay they cross'd and merrylie met,
> Fal lal etc

The bride and bridegroom, the bridesmaid and her sweetheart, and the
convivial old folks might be seated in the foreground, and behind them the
dancing groupe and the fidlers [*sic*] might appear.'

All this Wilkie included in the much later *Penny Wedding,* though it
was not destined for George Thomson. It is clear that Thomson, collector,
preserver and improver of Scotland's traditional folk songs was urging
Wilkie to undertake a complementary activity. He may have planned to
use Wilkie's pictures for illustrations, may have hoped to find in him
indeed a visual collaborator like David Allan, Thomson's old colleague at
the Trustees' Academy who had provided many lively drawings for the
Scottish songs. The position is complicated by the fact that Thomson's
elaboration of what he hoped Wilkie would paint for *Muirland Willie*

seems actually to have been based on one of Allan's illustrations to the same poem (N.G.S. D430).

Wilkie's belated response to Thomson, or to Thomson jointly with Allan, seems to have been to reach back to the eighteenth-century Scotland of Burns, Allan, and his own childhood memory. His *Penny Wedding* costumes are reconstructed versions of late eighteenth-century dress and his musicians, based on representations from the life by David Allan, are Niel Gow and his brother Donald.[10] Niel Gow, legendary in his own lifetime, was the Duke of Atholl's retainer, and died in 1807. Like Thomson's Scottish song collection Wilkie's *Penny Wedding* is an act of conservation of a tradition. Conservation is never thought of until one is losing or has actually lost something, and thus *The Penny Wedding*, unlike *Pitlessie Fair*, is not seen as happening 'now' but 'then' in some only just mislaid past when there were still fiddlers of genius about.

When Wilkie received Thomson's letter in July 1807, he was already the recipient of a slightly earlier, not dissimilar letter of 12 May, from the writer John Galt, enclosing, Galt later claimed, a copy of his poem *The Penny Wedding*.[11] This poem, eventually published in 1833, with a dedication to Wilkie, is a description of a wedding given as if verbatim by one of the guests, and is far indeed in spirit from the delightfully innocent conceptions of Wilkie and George Thomson. The bride is a sloven, the bridegroom a blockhead who drinks himself into a stupor, the guests all a 'hempy' or rascally set. Galt was probably mistaken in supposing that he himself had provided Wilkie with the germ of the *Penny Wedding*. Conservation and moral satire are to a certain extent mutually exclusive, for one either scorns and jeers, or preserves with affection and nostalgia, but not both. Galt was writing in an older tradition. The license of the wedding celebrations had always tended to break the bounds of decency, erupting in scenes of noise, combat and seduction, all gleefully described by the older ballad writers. Kirk Sessions record the Kirk's long, and apparently rather futile struggle to suppress or put in order these licentious Penny Weddings. The inevitable saturnalia seems to have broken out again regardless, and Walter Scott's first case as a young advocate was to defend a very minister of the Kirk charged with drunkenness and 'toying' with a 'sweetie wife' at a Penny Wedding.[12]

The domestic minded Wilkie, and Thomson who had implored Burns that the muse might always go decent, cannot have wished to see all the facts of the saturnalia exposed. They wanted to remember charm and spirit and not bawdiness and riot. Thomson's pleas to Burns for liveliness without indecency, and his enrolling of Haydn and Beethoven to embellish the native Scots tunes with foreign symphonies and accompaniments are analogous activities to Wilkie's elimination of the older cruder features of Penny Wedding celebrations—the excessive guzzling and drinking, the drunkards vomiting, and lewd asides—and his embellishment of the scene with some of the sentimental nostalgia of Greuze (whose work Wilkie probably knew in prints and may have seen when he visited France in 1814). It

15. Alexander Fraser's *A highland sportsman* painted in the Wilkie
manner by an artist who had acted as his assistant (*cat.15*)

is impossible for us to say categorically that Wilkie's record is 'untrue' for
feelings and memories are part of the ultimate truth about any past festive
occasion, and the earlier writers may have been just as selective in con-
centrating upon the ludicrous and disgusting aspect of the feast as Wilkie
in choosing the touching and attractive. Truth is one of the imponderables
inherent in attempting to provide the meaning as well as the outward facts
of an occasion. In *Pitlessie Fair* the simple difficulties of painting a record of
so much that was actually happening were sufficient for Wilkie without
introducing the subjective elements of meaning, value or understanding
into the celebration. However he was evidently thoroughly conscious, by
the date of the *Penny Wedding,* of the desirability of providing, along with
the facts, a sense of their age and their continuation, of the patina given by
time and memory to frequent ritually repeated past events.

Besides the poem of 1833 Galt wrote another description of a *Penny
Wedding* with a mood as tenderly retrospective as that of Wilkie's picture.
'The auld carles[13a] kecklet with fainness, as they saw the young dancers;
and the carlins[13b] sat on forms, as mim as May puddocks[13c] with their
shawls pinned apart to shew their muslin napkins. But, after supper, when
they had got a glance of the punch, their heels shewed their mettle, and
grannies danced with their oyes[13d] holding out their hands as if they had
been spinning with two rocks'.[13e] This—if one can understand the language—is very much like Wilkie's *Penny Wedding.* It describes a function
supposedly of 1807, but it was written in the novel *Annals of the Parish*
published 1821. Thus it follows the exhibition of Wilkie's *Penny Wedding*

16. Orchardson's *Queen of the Swords* of c.1877 is reminiscent
of Wilkie's *Penny Wedding*, exhibited at the London
International Exhibition in 1874 (*cat.18*)

in 1819, and it looks as though Galt's modified attitude towards the
wedding celebration may actually have been caused by seeing the Wilkie.

Whereas Wilkie's *Penny Wedding* is easy to understand, Galt's is, for a
southern reader without a dictionary, nearly incomprehensible because
written in a foreign language, and in fact Galt is not much read south of the
border. The barrier of language was something of which Thomson was well
aware. 'The English becomes every year more and more the language of
Scotland' he wrote to Burns in 1792. By 1822 he was weeding out or
changing songs in the 'broad Scottish dialect which are of a cast rather
vulgar' because the young now had lost 'all the partiality of their predecessors for songs in broad Scotch, considering the speaking of the dialect
to be vulgar and accordingly it is scarcely practiced except by old-fashioned
people and those in low life'.[14] Scots speech then in Thomson's opinion, is
old-fashioned, and modern improvement in polite manners is reducing its
incidence except amongst the old and low.

That the English form of speech was essentially modern and the Scots
language ancient was a belief Wilkie also shared. Burnet describes how
Wilkie listened with relish to a fellow countryman quoting stanzas from
Ramsay's poem *Christ's Kirk on the Green*—a poem about traditional
wedding celebrations—which English listeners found as incomprehensible as Chaucer. 'Wilkie said it was like one of the merry-makings of
Teniers, and might be translated into painting but not into modern
English, without losing the character of the subject and force of the language.'[15] In other words, painting can transcend the language difficulty
whilst preserving all the strength and patination of antiquity appropriate
to the subject matter. But what may we ask, is the pictorial equivalent to
the vernacular speech? Another Scottish painter present on the same

17. The Fife-born Wilkie's image of highland life, his *Death of the red deer* painted after a visit to Blair Atholl (*cat.4*)

18. The Duke of Atholl's Keeper, John Crerar, painted by Landseer at Blair Atholl, seven years after Wilkie's visit to Blair (*cat.11*)

19. Ramshackle *Highland interior* by Landseer, inspired by Wilkie's
Scottish interiors (*cat.12*)

occasion, explained this by saying that 'things familiar as household words
lost a great deal of their richness from want of the deep-toned glazings
antiquity gave them'. It is thus clear that the rich translucent surface, the
glazings and deep shadows of Wilkie's *Penny Wedding*—qualities not
present in the brashly coloured *Pitlessie*—are there for a purpose. They are
to remind one that this celebration is traditional and that it is very old. It is
not set amongst the modern or the polite but amongst what Thomson
would have called 'vulgar' people in 'low life' in whose habits the last
vestiges of what is ancient Scottish tradition as opposed to modern English
innovation, have taken refuge.

Between the lowlands and the highlands of Scotland there is a cultural divide. Language, custom, social organisation and history separate
the two regions. Wilkie's Scottish tour of 1817 took him into northerly
places which he had never visited before, and one outcome of this trip was
The death of the red deer (*cat.4*), painted a few years later in 1821. The
behaviour of civilised social beings had always hitherto supplied the
subject matter for Wilkie's art. The appeal of the highlands to the south, on
the other hand, was the appeal of the primitive and wild. For wildness, the
civilised Wilkie was perhaps, at this stage, ill-equipped. How could Jane
Austen have coped with expounding the nature of Scott's hero, Rob Roy

MacGregor? Since the highlands were to the Fifeshire Wilkie territory as foreign as Italy, Spain, Ireland and Syria, he grasped at some of the most obvious points—tartan, bagpipe music, and a propensity for slaughtering red deer. These, in novels from Scott's *Waverley* up to Compton Mackenzie's *Monarch of the Glen,* have been, and are still, made prominent features in most portraits of the highlands. The human figures in his picture, are, for Wilkie, curiously disengaged from each other, as if he did not know what they were thinking or for exactly what purpose they were assembled—and probably he did not.

To Landseer, who used Wilkie's *Death of the red deer* as a jumping-off point for his own portrait group of the Duke of Atholl and his retainers at the death of a deer, and for whom human psychology was a fairly unimportant pictorial ingredient, the wild and primitive came more naturally. Landseer had a better understanding of the anti-civilised aspect of highland life—at least as the southerner wished it to be interpreted. Animals, whom he preferred to humans as foci of attention, have behaviour without civilisation. Here again, however, Landseer was developing further an aspect of Wilkie's art, for Wilkie's perceptive and accurate descriptions of canine behavioural patterns within human civilisation almost certainly made a strong impression on Landseer. Lastly the mix of odd furniture, utensils, baskets, cooking pots and drinking vessels which Wilkie, from the *Village Politicians* on to the *Penny Wedding* was accustomed to stack and strew around the floor and shadowy recesses of his ancient cottages and barns, or suspend, half glimpsed, from dark rafters, provided Landseer with the picturesque vocabulary of his highland scenes. The same of course applies to Scottish artists such as Simson and Fraser, but in their case, a painterly technique also deriving from Wilkie, makes the debt more obvious.

Towards the end of the nineteenth century, the last ember from Wilkie's scenes of folk custom can be discerned in Orchardson's *Queen of the Swords (cat.18)* which, with its brown shadowy hall, its fiddler, and row of dancers in antiquated gowns of faded rose and brown and gold, is a final refrain—a mannered stylised refrain—of the nostalgic charm of Wilkie's *Penny Wedding.*

1. David Wilkie, *Pitlessie Fair* (*cat.2* detail)

2. David Wilkie, *Duncan Gray* (cat.22)

1. Cunningham vol.1, p.24.

2. I am grateful to Hugh Cheape of the National Museum of Antiquities for his helpful comments on the construction and materials of the houses in *Pitlessie*.

3. Alexander and John Bethune, *The fate of the fairest* in *Tales of the Scottish Peasantry* London and Glasgow 1884, p.61 (first published in two vols in 1838 and 1843).

4. I am grateful to Mr Boag of the United Services Museum, Edinburgh Castle, for information on recruiting parties and early nineteenth-century Scottish regimental uniforms.

5. Geikie's drawings of kitchens are in an album in the Prints and Drawings Department, NGS.

6. Letter to Perry Nursey of 5 November 1817, The British Library, Department of Manuscripts, MS Additional 29,991.

7. Quoted in J. Cuthbert Hadden, *George Thomson the friend of Burns His Life and Correspondence* London 1898.

8. National Library of Scotland, MS 9835 f.17-18.

9. J. Cuthbert Hadden op. cit. (note 7).

10. See Allan's *Highland Wedding at Blair Atholl* on loan to the NGS from the Trustees of the late Mrs Magdalen Sharpe Erskine. The subject was also etched by Allan.

11. See I. A. Gordon, *John Galt, the life of a writer* Edinburgh 1972, pp.10-11 and p.151 note.

12. J. G. Lockhart, *The Life of Sir Walter Scott* Everyman edition of 1969, p.63. The offender was Mr McNaught, Minister of Girthon.

13. a) old men, b) old women, c) frogs, d) grandsons, e) a double-handed wheel such as is seen in the foreground of Wilkie's *Distraining* (*cat.37*) and which was in general use in Pitlessie in the 1790s, according to Wilkie's father.

14. J. Cuthbert Hadden, op. cit. (note 7), p.132.

15. John Burnet, *The progress of a painter in the nineteenth century* London 1854, p.193.

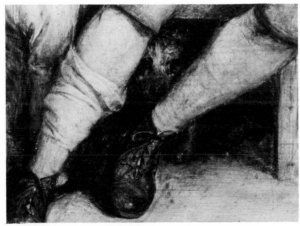

20. Wilkie's canine psychology would have appealed to Landseer. The unhappy dog in *Distraining for rent* (*cat.37* detail)

Character and Narrative

'SINCE THE exact resemblance of the face gives little pleasure, unless the mind is in a manner pourtrayed [*sic*]: it is not the *features,* but the *passions,* which the higher art is ambitious of transfusing, on to its canvass [*sic*].'[1] The words are Humphrey Repton's. He and Wilkie had been examining the paintings by Ostade in the Marquis of Stafford's collection. Repton felt, along with many of his contemporaries that the paintings of the seventeenth-century Netherlandish artists were deficient in their expression of the passions. One must remember that this word is not now used in the sense that Repton intended—a modern critic would probably talk of emotions or states of mind. 'If,' Repton continued, 'we examine the favourite subjects of either Teniers's we rarely discover any passion expressed in the human countenance, except the progress of intoxication— from the vacant stare of stupidity, to the utmost extremes of rage or brutal drunkenness', and Repton wound up his essay with a panegyric that quite obviously refers to Wilkie. To the superficial observer Wilkie's early pictures, *Village Politicians, The Blind Fiddler* and *The Rent Day* bore such an obvious resemblance to the work of Teniers that it was necessary for the more perceptive and penetrating critic to highlight the essential differences between Wilkie and his seventeenth-century predecessors. 'The Dutch pictures seldom embrace the varieties of action or expression, but are confined to brawls, merry-meetings, figures smoking, or playing at games of tric-trac; and where, if the general character is given, the colour or handling is never disturbed, by endeavouring to give a more intricate or correct definition of the passions.'[2] So wrote Wilkie's friend, engraver and fellow student, John Burnet. Lord Mulgrave perhaps put the matter most clearly when he told the artist Farington that 'He believed Wilkie would go beyond Teniers, Ostade & all who had preceded him, as he not only gave exquisitely the ordinary expressions of the human countenance but those of thought & abstraction'.[3] These two criticisms raise two points in Wilkie's treatment of character. That he is more subtle, 'intricate' and 'exquisite' in conveying inner states of mind than the seventeenth-century Dutch or Flemish painters, and that he is also more 'correct' in his definition of the passions. The idea of subtlety in the expression of mental states is easy to understand, within the context of the arts of painting, theatre, or even novel writing. 'A correct definition of the passions' on the other hand refers one beyond the arts to the world of science, and the accurate scientific study of emotion and behaviour. If a passion can be correctly defined it can, presumably, be incorrectly defined as well, so that any decision on whether the passions of Wilkie's *Village Politicians* are correctly delineated must be based on an appeal to some objective record of human behaviour. Wilkie himself did in fact as we shall see, have just such an objective standard in view.

About four months before Wilkie left Cults for London, another Scotsman, eleven years his senior, had also travelled south. This was Charles (later Sir Charles) Bell, a young surgeon whose work on the nervous system leading to his discovery of the distinct functions of the sensory and motor nerves was later to prove a major breakthrough in medical history. The young Bell was a gifted draughtsman who as a boy had been helped and encouraged by the Scottish artist David Allan, who called him affectionately 'brother brush' and lent him drawings after Raphael and the Antique, to copy. The relationship between his scientific and artistic skills was a matter of keen interest to Bell. He had already studied the classic works on the expression of the passions, by Descartes, Lavater and Lebrun, and brought with him to London the manuscript of a composition of his own, a *Treatise on Anatomy for the use of Painters* which was published in 1806 as *An Essay on the Anatomy of Expression in Painting* with illustrations drawn by Bell himself. It was his ambition, never realised, to be appointed Professor of Anatomy at the Royal Academy, for he was extremely critical of the bad drawing and anatomical ignorance of the British artists of the day. On 5 February 1806 he began a series of special lectures intended not for students of the medical profession but quite specifically for painters. Amongst the first of his students were Wilkie and his friend Benjamin Robert Haydon. Haydon indeed claimed that the lecture series was in fact suggested by Wilkie and the other students raised by his efforts.[4] Bell's students sat at little tables drawing skulls and skeletons, or listened to his discourse on the muscles of the trunk, demonstrated by the living model an 'admirable subject'. The general trend and content of the lectures was probably the same as that of the published *Anatomy,* and from its pages we can understand that Bell's chief concern was not static structure but the anatomy of the body in motion, and more particularly of the bodily motion induced by varying mental states. In his introduction he speaks of 'tracing the muscles of expression in their unexerted state, and of the changes induced upon them as emotions rise in the mind'. He regarded the standard artist's model fixed in a rigid pose as most

21. The ploughman, the weaver and the soutar argue over their paper in
Wilkie's *Village Politicians (cat.20)*

misleading to the student, 'In natural action there always is a consent and
symmetry in every part. When a man clenches his fist in passion, the other
arm does not lie in elegant relaxation . . . When a man rises from his seat in
impassioned gesture, there pervades every limb and feature a certain
tension and straining.' It is easy to see how helpful this kind of knowledge
would have been to Wilkie, engaged at that very moment with the
clenched fists, impassioned gesture and tension of the argument in his
Village Politicians. Bell believed that it was only through study of
anatomy that the artist could 'derive the true spirit of observation'. He
claimed that anatomy would not only enable the artist 'to give vigour to
the whole form it will, also, teach him to represent certain niceties of
expression, which, otherwise, are altogether beyond his reach'. It was,
surely, just these 'niceties of expression' this 'minuteness of observation'
that Wilkie was after, and the successful realisation of which marks the
Village Politicians off from the cruder treatment in *Pitlessie,* almost as
clearly as it marks the *Politicians* off from the work of Wilkie's pre-

22. Group psychology by Wilkie. Highland drovers and companions in
the background of *Village Politicians (cat.20* detail)

decessor, Morland, who had died in 1804 just before Wilkie came to
London. A comparison between a detail from the *Politicians* and a compar-
able detail of a Morland which includes an inn, adults, children with food
and a dog, shows that the closer one approaches a Morland the less the
faces have to offer. The lack of any expression, reciprocity or eye contact in
Morland suggests that he simply was not interested in the human relationships. Child, Dog, Barmaid, Traveller, they sink without trace into the
amorphous procession of similar characters in other pictures by Morland,
never asserting their unique identity as humans by a single individual
response, and barely even acknowledging each other's existence.

The important thing in the *Village Politicians* is the range of gestures
employed and the matching of them to positions of feet and arms as well as
facial expressions. There is no duplication. Each person is a distinct individual whose degree of involvement in the argument appears entirely appropriate to him as a person. What is more, the protagonists do not merely
gesture appropriately regardless of each other, like detached machines, but
interact like parts of one machine. The fingered chin of the old man, the
anguished outspread fingers of the interrupting man only exist because of
the points being emphatically rammed home on his palm by the young
firebrand speaker. In turn his own vehemence is undoubtedly heightened
by the hesitancy of the old man. Heads and shoulders are drawn together
like a knot by the intensity of the argument. Wilkie may seem to have
rather overdone his expressions, but this was inexperience. The second
group round the fire at the back, treated with greater quietness and

23. A detail from Morland's *Country Inn* lacks the psychological
interplay of Wilkie's picture

subtlety, shows where the way forward for him would lie. Despite the over
emphasis, on its first appearance this picture was recognised as unique,
and rightly so, for nothing like it as a study of group psychology in action
had ever been attempted before.

Cunningham identified the two figures next to the vociferous ploughman (indicated by the sock and coulter on the floor beside him), as a
weaver and a shoemaker.[5] It is not clear whether Wilkie told him the men's
trades, or whether he deduced them from pictorial evidence or simply
projected them onto the characters as a result of his own preconceptions.
Weavers were generally literate and had been particularly associated with
seditious activities in Scotland. Shoemakers also, another sedentary and
isolated occupation, were held to be politically opinionated. 'Every
genuine soutar of the old school is drouthy as the famous friend of Mr
Thomas Shanter, and will sit in the alehouse between clock and clock,
talking politics with whom he may. The soutar is universally a politician,
and commonly a radical.'[6] Although Cunningham's attribution of trades
may therefore simply have been an imaginative satisfaction of his own
expectations, it is nonetheless true that his confidence in allotting an
occupation to each figure arises out of Wilkie's own wish that his characters shall be seen as completely rounded human beings whose behaviour
in this given moment is part of an extended existence beyond the confines
of the picture. His trade does affect a man's personality, and Wilkie's
people are realised up to the point that the viewer is bound to enquire 'what
do they do during working hours?' Such a question hardly crops up before a

24. An exposition of the muscles of the face. Bored tenants
in Wilkie's *Rent day* (detail)

Morland, but it is deliberately posed, if only partially answered, by the
standards Wilkie set himself in the *Politicians*. It is a question that continues to be posed by a succession of later Victorian pictures, including
Frith's various panoramas, and Ford Madox Brown's *Work,* each character
in which accrued a virtual curriculum vitae in his creator's mind.

The Anatomy of Expression was published between the completion of
The Village Politicians and *The Rent Day*. The subject of *The Rent Day* is a
series of single figures or groups waiting to pay their annual rents to the
steward of a large estate. The steward on the left deals with the first man.
In the background those who have finished their business eat and drink.
Obviously the chief interest which can be extracted by the viewer from
such a situation is derived from observation either of the mannerisms of
people waiting, or from guesses, based on observation, of what they may be
thinking and feeling. Bell believed one could carry the spirit of anatomical
observation into 'the gaming house', 'the exchange' or 'the streets' and this,
in effect, is what Wilkie has done. The published *Anatomy* contained an
introductory and five following chapters. Of these, three were devoted to
the consideration of facial muscles and their relationship to states of mind.
Bell's concentration on the facial muscles is echoed by Wilkie's *Rent Day*.
The latter is indeed almost a catalogue or encyclopedia of the odd things
faces can do, coughing, arguing, gnawing the end of a stick, grimacing
with effort, swallowing food. These certainly are not 'passions' but they
are extraordinarily precise renderings of facial movements which most
painters had hitherto ignored. Hazlitt singled out Wilkie's coughing man
as a triumph of art.[7]

Bell was careful to distinguish between expressions of emotions in
animals and men. The animal's facial movements were, he believed,

25. Wilkie's *Blind fiddler* illustrates the interrelatedness of the arts. The child mimic is an embryonic Wilkie, whose drawing is pinned to the cupboard behind him (*cat.19*)

simply the necessary accessories to its actions at any given moment, whereas facial changes in human beings constituted a natural language of signs, a 'mode of communication'. 'There are even muscles in the human face to which no other use can be assigned than to serve as the organs of this language.' To the second part of this view Wilkie would undoubtedly have assented (though his treatment of canine expression throughout his career suggests that he regarded dogs as well able to communicate their feelings). The natural language of the face was as he saw it the link his painting maintained with both the connoisseur of art and the artistically uneducated person. 'By the human countenance . . . we are guided in our every-day intercourse with our species; and by this let the painter find light to his art.'[8]

The Blind Fiddler which followed the *Politicians* and preceded *The Rent Day,* is more unified as a narrative than either. It does not have either the discrepancies between the exaggerated and muted presentation of character seen in the *Politicians,* or the cataloguing attitude of *The Rent Day.* The father, facing us in the centre of the picture is another shoe-maker, representing on this occasion the musical, rather than the political tendencies of soutars. 'Every soutar is "musical"; at least a timber-tuned member of the genus never fell under our own eye. He beats his soles to time, and at every strain of the lingle, he is heard groaning out a strain of melody.'⁹

The small boy on the far right who silently copies the fiddler's movements was regarded by Hazlitt as simply a joke and 'a very bad one'. Luckily we know from Burnet's record that this was not exactly what Wilkie meant. 'I have considered him (the small boy) an imitating genius in embryo; that drawing over his head, wafered on the *amory* (i.e. cupboard) door, is a specimen of his pictorial propensity; it is a figure representing the Pretender, with his highland claymore.'¹⁰ Wilkie here is using imitation in a dual sense, to refer both to the child's impersonation of the fiddler and also to his ability to copy people and objects in a pictorial way. It seems clear that he felt the two skills were related to each other. For this belief, he had of course, very authoritative backing. Aristotle, on whose poetic criticism much eighteenth-century British art theory rests, had held that human beings were innately imitative, that when young they learnt their first lessons by imitation, and that they also enjoyed viewing works of imitation. Equally innate was the appreciation of music and rhythm. A work of imitation might well be a painting, but it could equally be based on language, as in a poem or a theatrical representation. Even dancing and music were counted as imitative arts. Wilkie's *The Blind Fiddler* is thus a representation by means of one of the imitative arts of the connections between them all, and of their appreciation even by the ignorant or very young. The fiddler's music, the soutar rhythmically snapping his fingers to the baby, who responds to his father's rhythm rather than to the fiddler direct, the naughty mimicry of the small boy, and the crude specimen of child art, are all parts of a whole. It does, however, seem likely that Wilkie's interest in the concept of the imitative arts was not merely intellectual but was based very firmly on his own personal experience. Like the child in his picture he was a painter and, by all accounts, an excellent mimic as well. Like the child in the picture, who is perhaps about seven years old (his age is indicated by his missing front teeth), one of Wilkie's early drawings was also of a soldier, copied from the print Sir John Sinclair had sent to his father when the artist was about six. All his friends' anecdotes and reminiscences enforce the notion that Wilkie had no verbal speed or aptitude. He was slow and repetitive in speech, falling back on absurd mannerisms such as his 'Well really' when hustled; he never saw the point of verbal jokes, and failed to appreciate puns even when they had been explained to him. Experience came to him and he communicated this experience in another manner than through language. When he first came to London and began to move in high society he appeared uncouth and awkward but this wore off with remarkable speed.

26. Self-portrait of Wilkie as one of his own
    Village Politicians (*cat.20* detail)

27. Self-portrait of Wilkie as a servant girl in his
    Blind fiddler (*cat.19* detail)

28. Wilkie painted by himself c.1804 for comparison
    with figs. 26 and 27 (*cat.1*)

By sharp observation Wilkie picked up the ability to imitate and *act* the part of a well bred man, an accomplishment Sir George Beaumont saw him practice with success in the space of a single dinner party.[11]

Early on in his student days Wilkie became accustomed to drawing his own hands and face from reflections in a mirror, using either his right or left hand to make the drawing. This habit, probably begun because there was no life model at the Edinburgh Trustees' Academy, he continued when he moved to London. Haydon, arriving to breakfast with Wilkie was a little startled to find his host stark naked, making a life drawing, in front of the mirror. Another visitor found him in the costume of an old woman, and his Scottish landlady on one occasion thought he must be weeping, he was making such odd faces at the glass. This exploitation of his own features was not confined to mere exercises or practice. The standing village politician in the group round the table was a likeness 'much overcharged' of Wilkie himself. He appears again his early historical picture of *Alfred in the Neatherd's hut,* and the hands of all the adult characters in *The Blind Fiddler,* including those of the fiddler himself, together with the expressions of the heads, are those of Wilkie. The servant girl indeed, on the far right, who watches the impudent small boy is, Burnet says, 'the strongest likeness we possess of Wilkie when a young man',[12] and a comparison of this head with that of Wilkie's 1804 self-portrait does indeed show exactly the same features. Wilkie's friends, the engravers Raimbach and Burnet, were quite clear as to his reasons for including these dramatised self-portraits in his work. 'His own plastic features, studied in the mirror', said Raimbach, 'assisted his unrivalled power of expression on the canvas'[13] and 'The dexterity and knowledge he thus acquired when young were of the utmost importance to him, when he carried out his pictures of familiar life',[14] Burnet explained, 'as he found it was impossible to get his models to give him either action or expression'. Models other than himself he did indeed use, often his early friends or associates, Callander, Stewart and Macdonald, who posed for the *Village Politicians* and *The Blind Fiddler.* The elderly newspaper reader in the *Politicians* was an habitué of the eating-house in Poland Street where Wilkie and Haydon used to dine. *The Blind Fiddler* was the real article, a musician accustomed to station himself in Oxford Street near Hanover Square, whose fiddling, Raimbach remarks 'was better than that of the generality of itinerant musicians'. It was however for what Burnet called 'a mixed expression' and which we should probably label a complex one, that Wilkie required his own face. He could not have explained, and nor could his model, whether friend, or hired professional, have interpreted the complexity of feeling in the servant girl at the extreme right of *The Blind Fiddler.* This inadequacy of the hired model to produce spontaneous subtle expression was of course one of the points Charles Bell had made in his book. But over and above this sound and comprehensible reason for using his own features, there does appear a possible second motive for self-portraiture, connected with Wilkie's own facility for mime and his equation of dramatic and painterly skills. It may

29. A Wilkie style of composition in three dimensions.
James Christie's terra cotta group *The dance*

well be that his conception of what expression would be appropriate to any character in a given situation was reached partly by trying it out himself, and that the reason for the viewer experiencing such conviction of the truth of Wilkie's gestures, and such empathy with his characters' movements is that these originated in the realm of the painters' own physical actions. His painting is really a form of acting, rather than a branch of literature, and it translated well, apparently, into staged tableaux, or even, as we can see, into small-scale sculptural groupings by his followers.

One by-product of Wilkie's habitual use of living models was an almost endless diversity in his characters. Each seems unique as in life and some, like *The Blind Fiddler* achieved that independent extra-pictorial life that one associates with the best of a novelist's creations, Jeanie Deans, Dominie Sampson or Mr Micawber, whom one can discuss as if they were people one knew. So Scott compares his own blind musician Wandering Willie, with Wilkie's fiddler, 'The man's face had been the instand before devoid of all sort of expression, going through his performance like a clown through a beautiful country . . . scarce seeming to hear the noise he was creating'.[15] Hazlitt, about two years earlier had felt the same, 'I know no situation more pitiable than that of a blind fiddler who has but one sense left . . . and who has that stunned or deafened by his own villainous noises'.[16] He too, as his footnote reveals, was thinking of Wilkie's picture.

The so-called rivalry between Wilkie and Bird, the Bristol painter, has been much discussed. Bird's *Country Choristers rehearsing an anthem for Sunday* (cat.23) was shown at the Royal Academy in 1810. By that date Wilkie had already exhibited *The Village Politicians, Blind Fiddler* and *Rent Day*. A careful scrutiny of Bird's painting reveals that so far from posing any real challenge to Wilkie, the picture is on the contrary a painstaking amalgamation of half understood lessons learnt by Bird from each of his rival's three most important paintings to date. The general structure and fall of light bears most resemblance to the *Politicians,* though the semi-circular extension of figure groups is nearer to *The Rent Day* and the musical element obviously derives from *The Blind Fiddler.* Much more important than structure, however, is Bird's use of gesture and expression. He has attempted Wilkie's wide and fascinating vocabulary of hand and facial movements without a true understanding of the unifying part that they can play in establishing the overall meaning. Wilkie paints an argument, a family listening to music, or a queue, and the bond of dispute, the bond of shared listening, or the bonding of boredom and anxiety, are made out in ways which, however disparate, underline our awareness that these are here shared, or communal activities. Bird on the other hand, creates out of the most unifying activity of all—shared music-making—a collection of particular and unrelated episodes. The same three paintings by Wilkie which influenced Bird seem to lie behind Lizar's painting of 1811, *Reading the Will* (cat.25). Lizars had of course been trained in Edinburgh at the same time as Wilkie. The Wilkie he knew was the farcical artist of *Pitlessie Fair* and he seems to have blended the crude characterisation of *Pitlessie* with the tightly knit grouping of the later pictures. Unlike Bird he grasped that the important thing was to show how people listen and react together to something which has significance for each of them.

The fascination of Wilkie's power to conjure up live thinking pres-ences, with a past and future, affecting each other by their behaviour—a quite different thing from the power to make a picture look physically, or deceptively real in terms of depth of solid form and tactile surface—worked curious changes on the most apparently unlikely artists. Turner, who, up until 1806, had largely been painting land or seascapes with rather small semi-distanced figures, the very next year produced, in acknowledged rivalry with Wilkie, a rural interior with close-up views of the faces of arguing of countrymen—a type of work he had never yet exhibited. There-after a number of paintings in which Wilkie-type themes and treatment are dominant witness to Turner's continuing curiosity about Wilkie's magic powers in evoking human relationships. In evoking space and atmosphere, Wilkie could not touch Turner, but there seem real grounds for supposing that the Turner of *The Harvest Home* (Tate Gallery) or *The Cobbler's Home* (cat.24) was not merely challenging the Wilkie of *The Village Festival* and *The Blind Fiddler,* but discovering for himself, by exercises in Wilkie's manner, how to manipulate a crowd of excited holiday makers, or unite the affectionate members of a family and their domestic animals in some simple activity. It is perhaps no coincidence that Turner's father, like that in *The Blind Fiddler,* is a cobbler. *The Harvest Home* incorporates seeming 'quotations' from *The Blind Fiddler, Blind Man's Buff* and *The Village Holiday,* suggesting that it must really post-date the 1811 and 1812 Academy exhibitions in which Wilkie showed *The Village Festival* and a sketch for *Blind Man's Buff.*

30. *Country Choristers* by Edward Bird, Wilkie's Wolverhampton-born rival (*cat.23*)

31. Turner's unfinished *Cobbler's home* is a response to the character studies of the cobbler's family in Wilkie's *Blind fiddler* (*cat.24*)

32. A device that helps to explain the story. The baby
with the house key in Wilkie's *Rent day* (detail)

It is time now to turn from the treatment of individual character to Wilkie's treatment of narrative. The stigma of literacy, Fry's accusation against Wilkie and his Victorian followers, is peculiarly bound up with the use of special little devices, clockfaces, books, posters, letters and scripts in general, mourning dress and clothes in general, new or shabby furniture, even food and drink or their absence, to convey narrative or biographical, that is, non-visual information. It is true that some of the Victorians used these devices to excess or with an ineptitude that called down the derision of such a critic as Thackeray, but both they and Wilkie would almost certainly have argued that in daily life one judges happiness or unhappiness, health and sickness, social status and personal tastes from expressions, complexions, clothes, and possessions—that is from visual information which is used by the intelligence to feed or amplify other sources of information—and that there is no reason why this habitual attitude of mind should be thwarted simply because one is looking at a painting. The real point is the originality and craft with which the painter deploys his schemes.

There is a marked difference between such informational devices as these and pictorial symbolism. Wilkie seldom, at any rate in the first half of his career, used much symbolism, but he was adept with the informational device. The impending auction of the baby's cradle in *Distraining* is an obvious example. One less obvious, at least to the present day, is the large key held by the baby in *The Rent Day*. We are fortunate in knowing from Carlyle, of all people, that this key was the long sought solution to a particular narrative problem. 'Wilkie had told him (Chalmers who reported this to Carlyle) how, in painting his *Rent Day*, he thought long and to no purpose, by what means he should signify that the sorrowful

Woman, with the children there, had left no Husband at home, but was a Widow under tragical *self*-management,—till one morning, pushing along the Strand, he met a small artisan family going evidently on excursion, and in one of their hands or pockets somewhere was visible the *House key.* "That will do!" thought Wilkie; and prettily introduced the House-key as *coral* in the poor Baby's mouth, just drawn from poor Mammy's pocket, to keep her unconscious little orphan peacable.'[17]

This story in turn suggests something about the way Wilkie arrived at his compositions. He did not aim to recreate the remembered appearance of a specific event once seen, and only seldom did he illustrate a given text. Rather, a situation arose in his mind as a possibility, and bit by bit was lent a real existence by the drawing together of different fragments of visual experience. When he visited the Elgin Marbles with Haydon, who was lost in rapture over them, Wilkie, on coming out, announced that he had been thinking up a new subject, involving little boys with a garden engine spraying each other with water whilst some took refuge in a green house.[18] There is no suggestion that he had ever seen anything of the kind, but that such an event, if the painter *could* make it exist, *would* be a good subject. The subject in embryo is thus not a visual effect, such as Whistler or the Impressionists would have approved, still less is it a pre-existing story, but merely a fragmentary glimpse of an activity or piece of behaviour from which a picture might be built. The little boys and the watering device were in fact never used.

I have claimed that Wilkie seldom resorted to symbolism. In Hogarth's paintings by contrast objects or furniture often contribute to his story, but frequently in a symbolic or emblematic way. The emblem is a sly aside, a private communication between the artist and spectator, an offer of information not available by these means to the characters within the pictured world and accessible to the viewer only because he knows the picture is not real. Wilkie generally avoided this, and his *Letter of Introduction* (*cat.21*), for instance, provides us with only so much knowledge of the two protagonists as they could, at that moment, achieve of each other, and by exactly the same means. This knowledge is partly natural and instinctive— what one calls knowledge of human nature—and partly social and the result of training. It was for instance easier for the contemporary spectator to identify social roles, weaver, cobbler, ploughman, in the *Village Politicians,* than it is for us. In the first instance, studying *The Letter,* we appraise the two men naturally by their faces, hands and postures, taking in their relative ages. Letters of introduction are seldom resorted to now, but even if one guesses that the subject may be 'hiring a servant' or 'a son asking for a loan' (both interpretations that have actually been made), one is not very far wrong. The interview situation is still a familiar one to most people. Beyond this point, one enters the zone of the social/historical in which the possession of libraries, busts, swords, Japanese jars, and the wearing of certain clothes in certain ways convey meanings that were part of the acquired social experience of the early nineteenth century. For us

3. David Wilkie, *The letter of introduction* (cat.21)

4. David Wilkie, *Distraining for rent* (*cat.37* detail)
5. David Wilkie, *The penny wedding* (*cat.3* detail)

33. Visual biography through furniture and possessions in Wilkie's
Letter of Introduction (cat.21)

again the interpretation of these aspects is not quite so easy. Most young
men no longer carry top hats, nor do elderly dilettanti swathe their crowns
in nightcaps, but these features are important because they extend our
awareness of the two people beyond the immediate moment into the
subtleties of social standing, family history and private tastes. The book-
case, bureau, bust, sword and jar, in fact the room as a whole, are a visual
biography of its particular occupant and owner.

His connoisseurship, and his literary and intellectual tastes are
revealed by the seventeenth-century Japanese Imari vase, the oriental
cabinet to the rear, the books, and the small bust, above the bureau, of the

34. *Answering an advertisement,* Stephanoff's satirical re-working of the situation in *The letter of introduction (cat.34)*

seventeenth-century philosopher Locke, author of the essay on *Human Understanding.*[19] His night-cap reveals him to be old-fashioned as well as elderly, since this was informal head protection for the wearer of a wig and by this date the younger men were wearing their own hair. His armchair of circa 1760–70 and his writing bureau of circa 1750–70 are similarly old-fashioned, being about forty years out of date. Wilkie discarded the modern French directoire chair and the mahogany bureau of circa 1800 which he had painted in his preparatory oil sketch, probably because they were too smart for the life style of the person he had in mind. In employing gesture, posture and possessions in this way Wilkie is not using, as Chalmers and Carlyle (men of language) seemed to suppose, a clumsy substitute for the spoken word but an independent, parallel, and sometimes more truthful language than speech. The interaction and play, even contradictory play, between these two languages is something that interested the early nineteenth century enormously. The unspoken language of physiognomy and behaviour frequently crops up as a topic in Hazlitt's essays ('Professions pass for nothing, and actions may be counterfeited; but a man cannot help his looks . . . A man's look is the work of years.'),[20] and there was a widespread belief that observation of character, and discrimination in its study was one of the pleasures of a civilised life. To this taste Wilkie's early pictures appeal and minister.

35. *They had been boys together,* Thomas Faed's anguished reworking of the situation in *The letter of introduction*

The Letter of Introduction was probably the most influential of all Wilkie's pictures. The flexibility of the relationship between and personalities of, the two protagonists, the mediating role of the dog, and explanatory character of the room setting allowed for almost infinite variations and rearrangements. A sketch for Stephenoff's entirely satirical *Answering an advertisement* (*cat.34*) of 1841 was sold in Paris in 1826 as *La Nouvelle Gouvernante* and attributed to Wilkie himself. Thomas Faed's large and elaborate *They had been boys together* of 1885 (now Durban Art Gallery, South Africa) abandons entirely the wry humour of Wilkie's original and concentrates on the heart-rending pathos of deviating fortunes. The neutral, if intrusive, letter has become a positive begging letter. In Russia Pavel Andreyevich Fedotov painted *A poor Aristocrat's breakfast* c.1850, which neatly balances satire and faint pathos. The jar, desk, bust and dog—which has turned into a very aristocratic clipped poodle—are adapted from Wilkie.[21] The interrupter is just coming in from a door to the rear. Pathos is dominant again in Redgrave's *Fashion's slaves* (*cat.35*) of 1846. This pathos, which is merely dormant in Wilkie—for we have no means of knowing quite what the result of the introduction will be or even how essential it may be to the young man's career—is cultivated by Redgrave into a full blown contrast between the 'haves' and the 'have nots', or capital and labour. The indolently reclining rich girl not only possesses all the objects of luxury surrounding her, but the life and health of the poor drudge confronting her. The downcast eyes

36. James Campbell's *Waiting for legal advice*, like *The letter of introduction* leaves the outcome of the interview in doubt (*cat.36*)

and arm positions of the sempstress are lifted straight from Wilkie's letter
bearer. The exquisitely painted gilt clock and china tea service, copied by
Redgrave from examples belonging to his patron John Gibbons[22] are more
overtly objects of possession and less—as in Wilkie—objects of biography.
There is no letter. The clock and the hour are the point at issue now
between the protagonists. The sempstress is late.

One of the most subtle of all the responses to *The Letter of Introduction,* and incidentally the only one in which full justice is done to the
complexities of the facial expressions and hands in *The Letter* is James
Campbell's *Waiting for legal advice* (*cat.36*). The physical arrangement

(44)

37. Courtship reluctantly received. An old man
proposing in Mulready's *Village buffoon*,
begun shortly after Wilkie's *Refusal* of 1814 (*cat.31*)

has been considerably altered but this is still a painting conducted on the
Wilkie principle, an open-ended situation, an incipient interview generat-
ing acute anxiety, but promising no precise resolution. The needs or hopes
or anxieties of the foreground pair are expressed in the movements of eyes
and brows and hands and in the restless tapping foot. Mr S.J.Downey,
Solicitor, in whose offices we appear to be, is no doubt in Victorian slang
terminology a 'downy' or astute cunning fellow. Mr Wylie—another wily
character—the auctioneer, and Downey are clearly in league, and it is
equally clear that the old man in the top hat will be the loser if they have
their way. Although the situation is partly explained by the text of the
poster, which serves the purpose of Wilkie's letter, or Redgrave's clock, the
ultimate point of the picture is the conflict of incompatible human needs
and expectations, a piece of psychological warfare, as in the Wilkie. The
main difference between Wilkie and the artists of a later generation,
Redgrave, Campbell and Faed is that he does not take sides or dictate the
reader's sympathies nor does he complain that social relations are largely
those of exploiter and exploited.

   Duncan Gray, of which the first version was painted immediately after
The Letter is one of the few pictures by Wilkie dealing with relationships

38. Hostility and courtship in Wilkie's friend Mulready's disturbing
Widow (cat.32)

between the sexes, and one of the few painted to an exact given text.
Duncan has come to woo Maggie who will not listen to him. Her parents
attempt cautious persuasion, meantime Duncan begins to change his
mind. The figures behind the door represent the 'we' or narrators of Burns'
poem—probably Maggie's brothers. The hands in this picture are almost
more telling than the faces and help the circular movement of appeal,
hostile denial, persuasion and gathering resentment which supply the
cyclical emotional phases of the story. Wilkie's friend, the painter
Mulready, sat for the figure of Duncan in the early spring of 1814.[23] The
subject seems to have made a strong impression on Mulready's mind for he
began his Diploma picture *The village buffoon* (*cat.31*) on a similar theme,
of courtship reluctantly received, the very same year. By 1815 it was
'½ done' and was completed in 1816.[24] Unlike Wilkie's pictures which were
normally self-explanatory, the subject of Mulready's painting seemed to
the Royal Academicians so obscure that Wilkie was called on to explain to
them that Mulready had intended to show an old man making unwelcome
marriage proposals to a young girl. A more complex painting, involving
varied reactions to courtship, which seems to relate both to Wilkie's
Duncan Gray and to his *Distraining for Rent* of 1815 was commenced by
Mulready in 1823, exhibited the following year, but returned to him
unsold. This was *The Widow* (*cat.32*), who, along with her forgetful

39. Wilkie's *Refusal,* an illustration to the courtship comedy
in Burns' song, *Duncan Gray*

younger children, readily succumbs to the confident approaches of a new lover. Only the eldest daughter, isolated in resentful gloom, remembers her father. The machinery that works character and situation is mainly of Wilkie's creation, but nothing could be less like Wilkie's innocent and optimistic confidence in basic human goodness than this embittered and disturbing evocation of faithlessness and family division. Mulready's own unhappy marriage broke up early for reasons never fully clear, and his grandson once described how the painter and his father began a quarrel that ended in a punch-up.[25] His own experience of family life was thus not a great success.

The first 1814 version of *Duncan Gray,* called *The Refusal,* became in due course the property of the collector Sheepshanks. There it would have been seen by the painter Charles West Cope who like his friend Redgrave and others of their generation had a fervent admiration for 'the venerated Wilkie'. Sheepshanks used to give Wednesday dinners at which Mulready, Leslie, Landseer and Cope himself were frequent visitors. Cope's own painting *Palpitation* (*cat.33*) exhibited in 1844 and also acquired by Sheepshanks, proves what close attention he had paid *The Refusal,* particularly to the motif of the figures behind the barely open door. He himself said that the painting represented 'A young lady waiting for her letter, while the postman and servant are gossiping on the doorstep'.[26] It is fairly obvious the letter in question is a love letter, possibly a clandestine one. The

40. Cope's *Palpitation*. A girl waits for her love letter while figures gossip
behind the door in a manner reminiscent of Wilkie's *Refusal* (cat.33)

horsewhip and animal skull in the hall suggest some sinister paternal
authority, at least to the modern viewer, but one must not forget that we
are looking in on an age in which every upper middle class wall bore its
shooting trophies, and every hall stand an array of sticks and whips, and
these may have no special significance.

The type of narrative and psychological painting created by Wilkie is
remorseless in its demands on the painter to occupy each second of his

41. Differing emotional states evinced by the mother, father, and neighbours in Wilkie's *Distraining for rent* (cat.37)

waking life in watching and remembering incessantly every visual detail in the behaviour of those about him—and Wilkie scarcely had a life outside his art—for if he does not, there will be nothing to supply the gestures and expressions of his painted characters but a horde of convenient stereotypes collected from memories of other people's pictures. The stereotype is convenient to the artist because it involves him in no effort. Equally he can be sure his public will know what is meant. Gesture in art thus becomes a kind of semaphore code which, if trained, we can understand, without for a moment supposing that this semaphore resembles the kind of arm movements normal people produce during their passages of communication with each other. It was Wilkie's belief, and the belief of many critics at the time, that truthful gesture—in contrast to the semaphore I have described —would not merely also be understood by the observer but would strike him with an extra force of conviction simply because its truth was recognisable. Hazlitt cites the case of the actor Kean, playing Richard in his last struggle, and borrowing his action from 'seeing the last efforts of Painter in his fight with Oliver'.[27] The process of observation, recall and—most important—re-use of the observed material in a proper context, is exactly that which underlies the paintings of Wilkie. The struggle to discard stereotype is now perhaps, and maybe has in the past nearly always been an essential force in art history. But the nineteenth-century faith in observation against all received precedent seems to have a peculiar character of its own. Wilkie's mentor, the surgeon Charles Bell, had began by assuming the appearance of a madman, made a conventional drawing, visited a madhouse, saw that his drawing bore no resemblance at all to real mad men, and began again on a new drawing.[28] In the last edition of his *Anatomy of Expression* he performed the same critical comparison between Raphael's treatment of the mad boy in *The Transfiguration* and the muscular spasms of actual epilepsy—a comparison that seems to have struck Holman Hunt as particularly important, for he quotes it extensively in his *Pre-Raphaelitism*. Bell's scientific approach to the depiction of human action and behaviour thus provides a link connecting Pre-Raphaelite painting with the art of Wilkie some forty years earlier.

Naturally, for the artist, insistence on truth of gesture will be easier to satisfy in depicting scenes with a low emotional key than in scenes of great emotional intensity or crisis. The games or squabbles of children, the movements of boredom or impatience, or the purely physical motions of a man coughing are seen often enough every day, and Wilkie's early genre pictures are all concerned with such trivial everyday actions. But what is the painter to do when dealing with madness, grief, suicidal despair? Not only does he hardly ever see people in such states, but when he does, the chances are that his own personal involvement in the situation will be too great for any detached artistic observation. How then is an artist such as Wilkie, able to paint a *Distraining for Rent*? In solving this problem Wilkie would appear once more to have looked to Charles Bell for guidance.

In his lectures to artists Bell had discussed such matters as 'a woman fainting from weakness on losing or finding her child'. In his book he also considered languor, faintness, sorrow, bodily pain, laughter and weeping, joy and discontent, wonder, astonishment, fear, terror, horror, despair and madness', and the muscles brought into play by each emotion. Because his subject matter straddled the boundaries between physical anatomy and mental psychology, Bell needed to define his emotional headings before detailing their effects. His definitions of 'despair', 'horror' and 'relaxation of languor, faintness and sorrow' do seem to account very precisely for the mental and physical states of the father, the neighbours in the centre, and the fainting mother, respectively, in Wilkie's *Distraining for Rent*. Following Bell's terminology, we see that the father is in despair. 'Despair is the total wreck of hope, the terrible assurance of ruin having closed around beyond all power of escape.' As a result, 'The eye is fixed, yet he neither hears nor sees aught, nor is sensible of what surrounds him . . . in all pictures of despair on inconsolable and total abandonment of those exertions to which hope inspirits and excites a man, forms an essential feature.'

The neighbours express horror. 'Horror . . . is less selfish, less imbued with alarm (than fear or terror), more sympathetic, having in contemplation the feelings of others . . . We are struck with horror even at the spectacle of artificial distress, but it is peculiarly excited by the danger or actual suffering of others.' In its effects, 'Horror is full of energy. The body is in the utmost tension.'

The mother experiences languor, faintness and sorrow. 'In sorrow, that general languor which we have now described pervades the whole countenance. The violence and tension of grief, the agitations, the restlessness, the lamentations, and the tumult, have, like all strong excitements, gradually exhausted the frame.' As a result, 'lassitude of the whole body, with dejection of face and heaviness of the eyes, are the most striking characteristics. The lips are relaxed and the lower jaw drops; the upper eyelid falls down and half covers the pupil of the eye'. These are the three main emotions experienced and displayed in *Distraining*. For the bailiff and his assistants, who are simply doing their job in a state of calm indifference towards the distress created, Wilkie obviously needed no assistance from Bell. In 1812 Sir George Beaumont had told Wilkie 'Deep pathos, although I think you are quite equal to it, you do not appear to aim at',[29] and the casual assumption seems almost to have operated as a challenge to the artist to produce a scientifically exact description of three very precisely distinguished states of pathos which would also be capable of stirring up the most powerful degree of sympathy in the spectator.

There was as it happened, a remarkable consensus of opinion on the truth of the characterisation in *Distraining for Rent* and all of the following independent comments stress exactly the same points.

> In such scenes as the *Distress for Rent* he never falls into caricature . . . but, with all the energy of expression, remains within the bounds of truth.[30]

> Every figure appropriate, natural, and telling: not an over-acted expression.[31]

> Wilkie takes no side but that of our common nature . . . We have here no hysterical passions—no shaking of fists against the heavens . . . as some melodramatic genius might have done.[32]

Nature and truth are thus recognised in the very bounds Wilkie has set, his control, his lack of hysteria, his rejection of a violent but entirely artificial emotional convention such as we mean by 'caricature', 'overacting', or 'melodrama'.

Equally common was the compulsive empathy experienced by the nineteenth-century viewer. 'What an immediate hold it took of us! How that sad family was in our mind for days after, and how we found ourselves wondering if nothing could be done for them! It is just about as difficult to bring the mind to criticise it, as it would be to occupy ourselves in thinking why or how we were affected, if we were ourselves to witness the scene in actual life . . . How strange! We never saw these poor sufferers, and we know they have no actual existence; and yet our hearts go out to them.'[33]

The mystery and fascination of this extraordinary pictorial hold, together with the possibilities it appeared to offer for changing the viewer's moral outlook, were as we shall see what most attracted the didactic Victorian artist Redgrave in the 1840s.

1. Humphrey Repton, *Observations on the pictures by Adrian Van Ostade in the Marquis of Stafford's collection* in John Britten, *Catalogue of the pictures belonging to the Most Hon. the Marquis of Stafford, in the gallery of Cleveland House* London 1808.

2. John Burnet, *Practical Essays on various branches of the fine arts to which is added a critical enquiry into the principles and practice of the late Sir David Wilkie* London 1848, p.101.

3. *The Diary of Joseph Farington* ed. Kathryn Cave, vol.3, Newhaven and London 1982, p.2993.

4. *Life of Benjamin Robert Haydon* ed. Tom Taylor, 3 vols, London 1853, vol.1, p.43.

5. Cunningham, vol.1, p.113, but it should be observed that in vol.3, p.501 he refers to them as 'the ploughman, the joiner, and the weaver'.

6. Sir Thomas Dick Lauder, *Etchings illustrative of Scottish character and scenery by the late Walter Geikie, RSA*, Edinburgh 1841, p.9.

7. William Hazlitt, *On the works of Hogarth— on the grand and familiar style of painting* in *Lectures on the English comic writers* first published 1819. 'What strikes the mind is the difficulty of a man's being painted coughing, which here certainly is a masterpiece of art'.

8. Cunningham, vol.3, p.162.

9. Sir Thomas Dick Lauder, op. cit. (note 6), p.9.

10. John Burnet, *The progress of a painter in the nineteenth century* London 1854, p.31.

11. *The Diary of Joseph Farington* ed. Kathryn Cave, vol.7, Newhaven and London 1982, p.2716.

12. John Burnet, *Recollections of my contemporaries. The early days of Wilkie* in *The Art Journal* 1860, p.237.

13. *Memoirs and recollections of the late Abraham Raimbach Esq., Engraver, including a Memoir of Sir David Wilkie, R.A.* ed. M. T. S. Raimbach, London 1843, p.156.

14. John Burnet, *Practical Essays* op. cit. (note 2), p.105.

15. Sir Walter Scott, *Redgauntlet,* first published 1824, vol.2, chapter 13.

16. William Hazlitt, *Why distant objects please* in *Table Talk,* first published in two vols 1821 and 1822.

17. Thomas Carlyle, *Edward Irving* in *Reminiscences* ed. Charles Eliot Norton, first published 1887, Dent edition of 1972, p.215.

18. *Life of Benjamin Robert Haydon* ed. Tom Taylor, 3 vols, 2nd edition 1853, vol.1, p.151.

19. I am grateful to Timothy Clifford for the identification and dating of objects within the picture.

20. William Hazlitt, *On the knowledge of character* in *Table Talk,* first published in two vols 1821 and 1822.

21. See pp.95-96.

22. I am grateful to the owner of Redgrave's painting for this information.

23. An undated letter from Wilkie to Mulready, in the Victoria and Albert Museum Library, contains a request for a sitting.

24. Mulready's Account Book, Victoria and Albert Museum Library, MS 1961/4463.

25. F. M. Redgrave, *Richard Redgrave, a Memoir* London 1891, p.278.

26. C. H. Cope, *Reminiscences of Charles West Cope* London 1891, p.165.

27. William Hazlitt, *On genius and common sense* in *Table Talk,* first published in two vols 1821 and 1822.

28. *Letters of Sir Charles Bell selected from his correspondence with his brother* London 1870. On 24 June 1805 Bell sent his brother a drawing of a madman. After visiting Bedlam he admitted 'I drew it on a theory, and I can find nothing like it in the cells of the madhouses. I mean to say so, and to show in what it is not mad . . .'.

29. Cunningham, vol.1, p.343.

30. Waagen, *Treasures of Art in Great Britain* 3 vols, London 1854, vol.1, p.375.

31. *Journals and Correspondence of Lady Eastlake* ed. Charles Eastlake Smith, 2 vols, 1895, vol.1, p.183.

32. Dr John Brown, *Notes on Art* first published 1846, reprinted in *Rab and his friends and other papers* Edinburgh 1884.

33. Ibid.

Modern Life

FRITH'S *Ramsgate Sands, Derby Day,* and *Railway Station* (*cat.45*),
Ford Madox Brown's *Work,* William Maw Egley's *Omnibus Life in
London* and George Elgar Hicks' *General Post Office* are all mid-Victorian
works of art which deal with modern life in a way that one can broadly
describe as celebratory or congratulatory. Richard Redgrave's *Seamstress,
Poor Teacher,* and *Fashion's Slaves,* Egg's *Past and Present,* Martineau's
Last Day in the Old Home (*cat.43*), Holman Hunt's *Awakening Conscience*
and Rossetti's uncompleted *Found* (*cat.65*), like the reverse of the same
coin, depict modern life as entailing serious social problems, errors and
injustices, and solicit the sympathies or batter the conscience of the
intended viewer. Both kinds of painting were rife during the 1840–60
period, nor are they so utterly dissimilar to each other as one might
initially suppose. The first class treats Victorian life comprehensively, in
situations where numerous individuals, who would not otherwise have
many personal contacts with each other, are assembled in one place. Here,
the image of the way individuals from different social groups interact
resembles sets of interlocking cogwheels, as in the mechanism of a watch,
deliberately stopped at a given moment, and opened, so that the positions
and relations of all its working parts are laid bare. The painting as a whole
celebrates the machine as a whole, whilst acknowledging that some individual parts (as we can see in Frith's *Railway Station* with its arrested

criminal) may be faulty and in need of replacement or repair. The second class of pictures ignores the machinery as a complete system in order to focus attention on one or another of the faulty parts.

The paintings cited above, whichever of the two classes they belong to, are unique to the mid-nineteenth century. Indeed, the very term Victorian painting seems to conjure up a mental image of something like Frith's *Railway Station*. Those features common to the Frith, Brown, Egley and Hicks paintings, their attitudes towards time, place, and change, social class and the individual, urban life, technology, fashion, visual accuracy and even pictorial finish, can be traced back to Wilkie's *Chelsea Pensioners*. In a real sense this was the first celebratory Victorian painting of modern life. Similarly, Martineau's and Redgrave's scenes of modern distress have a pedigree that returns to Wilkie's *Distraining for Rent*. The face and the reverse of the coin were both originally of Wilkie's minting.

Pitlessie Fair describes what for Wilkie was the present moment, although it is the past for us. So too, though in a different way, does the *Village Politicians*. *Pitlessie Fair* was an attempt to reconstruct the truth about an actual event. The *Politicians* is a synthetic work, presenting a fiction, albeit a probable fiction, with such a wealth of circumstantial evidence that it seems as if it must really have occurred just like that. 'The subject of your picture must be regarded as a fortunate one:' Wilkie's father wrote in 1806, 'political disputes and cabals are still popular in our villages among the lower classes.'[1] The political cabals to which he refers were probably the remnants of the Society of United Scotsmen founded in 1797 in order to agitate for universal suffrage and annual Parliaments. This society seems to have been particularly strong in Fife, and although such societies were suppressed by Act of Parliament in 1799, the United Scotsmen continued their activity in Fife on into the early years of the nineteenth century. After 1802, however, as Lord Cockburn pointed out in his *Memorials*, Jacobinism and sedition appeared far less serious threats than the more immediate possibility of invasion by the French. The *Village Politicians* therefore represents the harmless tail-end of those popular political movements generated by the French Revolution. The politicians are talkers, not doers, and there is no hint on Wilkie's part that the iron sock and coulter, brought in by the vehement young ploughman for their regular sharpening by the blacksmith, are really to be re-shaped as pikes and axes such as were forged at Stockbridge in Edinburgh, in 1794, by the 'Friends of the People'.[2] The ministers of the Church of Scotland who had contributed towards the *First Statistical Account of Fife*, were upholders of the status quo, and tended to attribute—apparently correctly—seditious activities to the sects of the seceders. Wilkie himself, as one would expect of a minister's son, was no advocate for political reform, and, when forced to drink success to it by his friend Haydon, qualified his reluctant toast with a 'but very moderate though'.

His painting was based on a didactic poem, *Scotland's Skaith* by Hector MacNeill, first published 1795, republished 1801 and thus itself a product of the post-revolutionary political climate. This rhyming tract was aimed at a double target, village jacobinism and alcoholism. To MacNeill politics were the lure but alcoholism was the baneful result.

> See them now in grave convention
> To mak a' things 'square and even';
> Or at least wi' firm intention
> To drink sax nights out o' seven

Small as Cults parish was, it had supported, at the date of *The First Statistical Account,* one inn and four licensed alehouses. The consequences of the change taking place in the country's drinking habits from beer or ale (which MacNeill approved as healthy) to whisky, were recorded with concern in 1791 by the minister of a nearby Parish, Saline, where an inhabitant had been killed by whisky and was carried away dead out of the public house. Anxious ministerial conversations on such topics as whisky and local political agitation had probably been familiar to Wilkie's ears throughout his childhood, and such familiarity would explain why he latched onto MacNeill's bad poem so eagerly, borrowing its title to give supporting dignity to his first exhibit at the R.A. in London, where hardly any of his viewers were at all likely to have read *Scotland's Skaith.* He shows us that the young ploughman is drinking whisky from a small measure in front of him, whilst the elderly man, faithful to earlier habits, drinks ale from a capacious jug beside him on the floor, but as handled by Wilkie this turns into a neat piece of social observation, a record of changes like those in *Pitlessie,* not an indictment.

The nature of argument is Wilkie's own real subject. Politics are simply the subject of his disputants. If Wilkie makes them argue on politics this is partly, one suspects, because in Fife at that date and for many years after, it was only 'the medium of white heat politics' that could, according to Alexander Bethune, be relied on to galvanise the country speaker to animated movement. 'Talk to them of religion, and they will put on a long face . . . confess that it is a thing of the greatest importance to all—and go away and forget the whole. Talk to them of education: They will readily acknowledge that its a braw thing to be weel learned . . . but they neither stir hand nor foot further . . . But only speak to them of politics, and their excited countenances and kindling eyes testify in a moment how deeply they are interested. If, moreover, you have anything new to tell them . . . the thing will serve them for a subject of conversation among their companions for weeks to come.'[3]

The 'new' was passed on either by word of mouth, or by the printed word in newspapers, which were distributed via the post office system. If argument is Wilkie's first subject, the sources and distribution of information are his second, and as in the move from ale to whisky, we are shown a changing pattern of communications. The customers at the ale house are divided into two groups, those of the foreground being the resident locals whose trades have already been discussed. Newsagents for the distribution of papers to individuals did not exist at this date, and it was normal for

42. The newspaper reader in Wilkie's *Village Politicians,* was a portrait of a regular customer at the tavern in Poland Street frequented by the artist (*cat.20* detail)

groups like MacNeill's and Wilkie's politicians to club together for subscription to a shared paper, and meet to discuss its contents.[4] MacNeill's politicians were readers of *The Edinburgh Gazeteer,* a violent opposition periodical, briefly published from 1793–4. Behind the main group in Wilkie's picture, disputing over national events presented to them in printed form and circulated from London or Edinburgh, is a second, subsidiary group, composed partly of locals and partly of highland drovers— itinerants who do not travel on the modern post roads which shift mails and journals, but along the soft cross country tracks that bypass tolls and link up markets. Whereas the foreground group dispute with anger and intensity, the drovers and their friends gossip gently, presumably of trysts and cattle prices, or other agricultural matters. The inn kitchen, picturesquely dirty and disorganised as all Scottish tourists of that period discovered to their cost, is thus a receiving point for two cultures with distinct and contrasting links of communication with the outside world. The complexity of the social observations and wealth of supportive detail remove Wilkie's picture quite as far from the inn scenes of Morland as Wilkie's handling of character and personal relations does.

The *Village Politicians* became the parent of the many Victorian paintings illustrating the postal service and the distribution and reception of news via letters and journals. The idea was re-shaped by Wilkie's friend, Benjamin Robert Haydon, in his 1831 *Waiting for The Times* (*cat.28*). Haydon had watched the creation of Wilkie's *Politicians* stage by stage in 1806 with an enthusiastic yet jealous curiosity. Occupied as his mind was in 1831 by the disputed Reform Bill and his own three letters on this subject to *The Times,*[5] it was natural that he should return in memory to

43. Walter Geikie's excited ale-house reader recalls the bespectacled man in Wilkie's *Village Politicians*

the first picture in which he had seen contentious political reform depicted through the reading of newspapers.

By a similar act of association Christopher North (Professor Wilson) in the *Noctes Ambrosianae* of 1829, when defending the freedom of the press, adverted to Wilkie. He was criticising the government as then composed 'partly of drawling dunces, who dole out a vast fund of facts, one and all of which have figured for weeks, months, years, in all the newspapers, metropolitan and provincial, and have ceased to be familiar to Wilkie's "Village Politicians".'[6] At first hearing Wilson only seems to be trotting out a trite comment on stale news in villages—'And news much older than their ale went round'—so that it takes one a moment to grasp his paradox—You expect village politicians to be badly informed, and Wilkie's, because Scottish villages are remote and backward, more so than most, but things are now turned the other way about. The villagers receive an up-to-date press and it is Parliament which has become a collection of ignorant village politicians. Wilson's use of Wilkie's picture to make this point rises of course directly out of Wilkie's own attempt to grasp contemporary issues, and his sensitivity towards the early signals of crucial social changes. The main difference between *Pitlessie* and the *Politicians* lies in the fact that the transition is now being presented from a point of view. This is the point of view of an elderly minister's son, and we may not like it. We may also suspect that there is a commercial element in Wilkie's choice of subject, but the fact of his keen awareness of these social changes remains.

44. Haydon's mix of news and radical politics, *Waiting for The Times,*
painted during debates over the Reform Bill, harks back to Wilkie's
Village Politicians (cat.28)

It is possible that Turner, whose interest in Wilkie's powers of characterisation has already been discussed, was irritated by what may have seemed a spurious bid for public attention by linking contemporary politics with rural genre. His *Village Blacksmith disputing upon the price of iron, and the price charged to the butcher for shoeing his poney* was planned as a competitor, or a rebuke—or both—to the *Village Politicians,* and was exhibited at the R.A. the following year, near, but not immediately next to *The Blind Fiddler.* The technical aspects of Turner's rivalry with Wilkie, centred on the problem of whether the *Blacksmith* was a brighter picture than the *Fiddler,* have attracted so much contentious discussion that nobody seems to have spared a thought for the relationship of Turner's subject matter to Wilkie's *Politicians.* Whilst the latter was on view at the Academy, Parliament was debating the very measure which must have given Turner his theme and title, the Pig Iron Duty Bill. This had been a budget announcement of Lord Henry Petty on 28 March, a proposal to defray interest and charges on the war loan by a tax of forty shillings per ton on pig iron, which he reckoned would produce £500,000. This was hotly disputed. Petty was told that the 'measure was pregnant with the most destructive effects to every branch of commerce, manufactures, and agriculture' and it was calculated that 'the additional expence on every horse employed in husbandry would be twelve shillings a year'. Turner must have read these debates, which his picture reduces to

45. Turner's *Village blacksmith,* who argues a current Budget measure with his customer, was painted to rival Wilkie's *Village Politicians*

their last absurdity at the level of an argument in the village forge. It is a joke, but an envious joke, at the expense of Wilkie's *Village Politicians*. It is also a somewhat enigmatic joke which leaves one uncertain how far Turner felt it proper to relate this kind of painting to topical politics. He may be telling us that all high political argument boils down, in the village, to its effects on one's own livelihood, or ironically pointing out that, however grandiose the title, in a picture one can only see, not hear, what is being said, or simply announcing, 'Whatever Wilkie can do in relation to current issues, I can do better'.

Part one of *Scotland's Skaith,* the poem from which Wilkie developed his *Village Politicians,* and verses of which he used again to explain the subject of his *Village Festival,* concludes with the roup (auction sale) of the alcoholic family's household property.

> Bond and bill, and debts a' stoppit,
> Ilka sheaf selt on the bent;
> Cattle, beds, and blankets roupit
> Now to pay the laird his rent;

Although Wilkie made no specific reference to these lines in connection with his *Distraining for Rent,* it is this image which underlies the picture, with the difference that the scene has now been moved south of the Border. In Scotland there had been no process for distraining since 1469. The Scottish process for removing goods from a defaulting rent payer is called poinding (pronounced pending) and the officials concerned are not those portrayed by Wilkie.[7] In *Distraining* we see the bailiff with two assistants,

46. Agricultural collapse at the end of the Napoleonic Wars, depicted in
Wilkie's *Distraining for rent* (cat.37)

who is preparing to provide the tenant with an official written notice of the
distress and an inventory of his goods to be seized.

Wilkie's sketch for his subject was executed early in 1814, following
the previous year's parliamentary debates on the reformation of the laws
relating to insolvent debtors, and the passage of three Acts, the *Insolvent
Debtors (England) Act* (53 Geo III c.102), the *Insolvent Debtors (England)
Act 1813* (54 Geo III c.23), and the *Insolvent Debtors Relief Act 1813* (54
Geo III c.28). The debates on the subject continued into December of 1813,
and the superiority of the Scottish over the English bankruptcy laws was
pointed out. Two of the Acts dealt with distraining and with the problem of
a debtor attempting to conceal goods in order to avoid distraint. The
parliamentary debates must have prompted a good deal of general talk
about these issues, and we know that Wilkie's friend Charles Bell, whose
brother wrote the classic work on the Scottish bankruptcy laws (*Bell's*

Commentaries), discussed the matter by letter with his brother in Edinburgh.[8] These debates provide the contemporary context for Wilkie's *Distraining*.

So far so good. We have authoritative reason for believing that Wilkie adopted this subject as an experiment to demonstrate 'that he was not to be estimated merely as a painter of *comic* scenes'.[9] To his dismay and surprise, at the private view of the R.A. his picture was spoken of as a 'factious subject' intentionally aimed at the landowning classes. Even Wilkie's old friend and patron Sir George Beaumont became 'very sore . . . and said Wilkie should have shown why his landlord had distrained; he might be a dissipated tenant'.[10] That is, Beaumont put a Hogarthian reading onto the subject, the logic of which runs as follows. When disasters occur someone is to blame. If the tenant is lazy his failure is his own fault. If he is not to blame then the landlord must be in the wrong. If the landlord is acting with cruelty the picture becomes an attack on landed proprietors. Years later, Wilkie's biographer Cunningham was to adopt precisely the same method of approach but reverse the reading. For Cunningham the tenant had quite patently been slack and inefficient for a long time before disaster actually struck. This landlord versus tenant see-saw is not, as we have seen, the only possible interpretation, but one that unhappily dogged the painting for some time. In the summer of 1815 it was innocently bought by the Directors of the British Institution, but the rumours of subversion in due course caught up with it again. The Directors became 'frightened' at supporting an 'attack' on landlords, and hid the picture in a dark lumber room where students washed their brushes, and it stayed there for seven years until Raimbach bought it in 1822, to engrave.[11] This history of suspected crime and punishment may amaze us now. Beaumont's indignation and the fright taken by the British Institution may seem inexplicable reactions to a picture that could move the gentle and sensitive viewer to tears, but Wilkie had in truth made a naive blunder, and its results were such as he ought perhaps to have foreseen. The *Distraining* like the *Village Politicians* was very precisely related to the political situation of the moment, and in touching on this situation, more especially touching it with such sympathy for the sufferers, Wilkie jarred a highly sensitive public nerve. The close of the Napoleonic wars had brought to an end the high wartime prices for corn which had hitherto given the farmers prosperity, and the ruined farmer was now no mere figment of Wilkie's imagination, but a bitter reality. No doubt the agricultural collapse, and the savage wranglings over the Corn Laws had in part suggested his subject to him. Precisely the same considerations were bound to affect the judgement of the viewer.

Wilkie's picture was intentionally topical but not, it would seem, intentionally polemical, for he was totally unprepared for the hostility he aroused. As time passed, and the political situation altered, the painting itself almost inevitably came to be seen in a different way, particularly in the late 1830s and 1840s when radical judgement approved the depiction of

47. Redgrave's *The outcast,* like *Distraining for rent* depicts the tragic disruption of family life (*cat.40*)

helplessness and exploitation.

Artists from Hogarth to Morland (whose *Comforts of Industry* and *Miseries of Idleness* (N.G.S.) do require the interpretation Sir George Beaumont mistakenly applied to *Distraining*), represent misfortune as something for which the sufferer is individually responsible, whereas Wilkie invented a flexible model for a new kind of distress scene in which sufferers are victimised by social and legal circumstances beyond their control. Raimbach's engraving was not popular—Wilkie had warned him it would not be—but it had at least made the subject familiar to the audience on the first night of Douglas Jerrold's play *The Rent Day,* 'a domestic drama in two acts, dedicated to David Wilkie Esq R.A.', first performed on 25 January 1832.[12] The rising of the curtain on the first act disclosed a tableau modelled on *The Rent Day.* At the end of the act the curtain dropped upon a second tableau.

> *Toby*: Blood-suckers!
> *Bullfrog* (The appraiser): One toasting-fork, one bird-cage, one baby's rattle!
> *Martin*: God help us! God help us! (buries his face in his hands. Bullfrog seats himself on bed and other characters so arrange themselves as to represent WILKIE'S Picture of DISTRAINING FOR RENT.)

Jerrold's play, with its open criticisms of bad absentee landlords and their brutal agents, and its references to the workhouse and emigration as the cruel fates awaiting the evicted family, suggests that since the first hostile reception of *Distraining,* society had in some manner adjusted itself so as to be able to accommodate criticisms of a kind that, uttered in Wilkie's day,

48. Martineau's *Last day in the old home*. Extravagance and debts
operating at a higher social level than in Wilkie's *Distraining*, but
with somewhat similar results (*cat.43*)

had appeared to threaten the stability of the whole structure. As a result
there is an element of complacent public breast-beating in the journalistic
reviews of mid-nineteenth century paintings of poverty, eviction, family
breakup, and emigration, that scarcely seems preferable to the British
Institution's deliberate suppression of *Distraining*.

Redgrave's Diploma picture *The Outcast* (*cat.40*) represents a kind of
hybridisation between the family disasters of Greuze and Wilkie's *Distraining*, which he would have seen on visits to the owner, Wells of Redleaf.
Collinson's *Emigrant's Letter* (*cat.39*) on the other hand, is an intentional
exercise in the Wilkie manner. The net effect of all its detail is one of rather
painful effort and anxiety, but the viewer is left uncertain whether this is
intended to convey the feelings of the letter-writing family in the cottage,
or whether the painstaking labour over details is not rather a means of
grace for the artist himself, an intrinsic virtue, almost a penance, independent of its pictorial results. Collinson's decision after 1850 to abandon

49. Thomas Faed's *From dawn to sunset* shows the varied reactions to tragedy in the home circle (*cat.42*)

the Wilkie manner for the 'Early Christian'[13] suggests that the Wilkie manner as he understood it, committed one to far more than a mere pictorial style; it entailed a philosophy of human behaviour, a view of religion, class, and social situation, even the adoption of a certain code of moral values. It could be applied to contemporary labourers in cottages but not to medieval saints in churches. Artists like the Scot Tom Faed, who played their own variations on Wilkie's Scottish farmhouse and cottage themes, have done much to establish the image of Wilkie as intrinsically a cottage painter. Faed's *The Poor, the poor man's friend* (*cat.27*) develops the aspect of *The Blind Fiddler* that is concerned with home and homelessness or comparative degrees of poverty. His *Forgiven* (*cat.41*) and *From Dawn to Sunset* (*cat.42*) explore tragedy and suffering within the rural family circle. Their relationship to Wilkie's work is easy to recognise. Less obvious is the relationship of Wilkie's *Distraining* to Martineau's *Last day in the old home* of 1862. But provided we do not allow ourselves to be blinded by Martineau's elevation of events onto an utterly different social level, amongst a family with far more wealth to squander and luxury to lose, we can see that the idea as well as the machinery by which it is presented is that of *Distraining for Rent*.

Unlike his previous pictures, Wilkie's *Chelsea Pensioners* describes a single moment of public and historical time. When the Bastille was stormed he was three years old. When France declared war on England in February 1793, he was seven. Thus throughout the crucial years of his later childhood, and on until he was nearly thirty years old, Britain and

50. Wilkie's *Chelsea Pensioners* celebrate the ending of a war that had lasted twenty-two years (*cat.38*)

France were almost continuously at war, with two short breaks, between 1802 and 1803, and again briefly in 1814 and 1815 before Napoleon escaped from Elba. We have seen how Wilkie's first major picture, *Pitlessie Fair,* acknowledges the presence of war in ordinary life. *The Chelsea Pensioners,* his masterpiece, is a celebration of the final victory that closed the series of events commencing with the French Revolution. It summed up and finished a chapter in Wilkie's own career as an artist, and it also provided a new opening, or departure point for the Victorian panoramas of modern life later produced by Frith. *The Chelsea Pensioners* contains both comedy and tragedy, it is genre and it is history, fiction and reportage. Upon the base of real events—for the battle of Waterloo *was* a British victory, such a Gazette *was* published, and at some point the news must have been brought to Chelsea—Wilkie has constructed a very persuasive fiction incorporating plenty of real Peninsula Veterans, and even—a fine touch—a real veteran army dog.[14] A moment's thought, as one scrutinises the various reactions of the pensioners and their families, will, however, reveal that we are not really seeing what did happen at that particular moment—contemporary observers were quick to point out that no-one eats oysters in June—but a pretence very carefully constructed to represent as broadly as possible the human implications of war and victory. Wilkie seems to be offering us unique individuals, but they also perform the roles

(65)

of universal types. It is interesting that the French artist Géricault, who saw Wilkie's *Chelsea Pensioners* in the studio, a year before it was publicly exhibited, was clearly not told (for, one must suppose, reasons of common politeness) what the real subject was. Ignorant of its particular historical significance for his own and Wilkie's nation, he interpreted it merely as *a,* not *the,* victory, and concentrated on responding to its aspect of universal truth, the rejoicing, the 'pathos like nature itself'.[15]

The Pensioners had a very long gestation period, from the moment in 1816 when the Duke of Wellington selected a study of old soldiers enjoying themselves outside a pub door to the moment in 1822 when it was sent to the Royal Academy. The exact point at which the Victory of Waterloo was introduced to control the situation is not known. We do know that by the end of 1818 Wilkie had made two very different oil sketches of the subject, and by 1820 he was beginning to put in the figure groups upon his large (though Géricault called it small) five-foot panel. By December of 1821 Wilkie had completed the human figures but was only commencing the background. (If what Géricault saw was this version—rather than one of the sketches—the human character and expression were the only aspects then available for comment). 'The background which will be Chelsea Hospital I am to paint from Drawings made upon the spot; and both that and the houses that come up to the figures are so well suited to my purpose that I mean to make a facsimile representation of them.'[16] This most crucial decision was adhered to, for though he admitted to Geddes in 1821 that he was having difficulty with the background houses, he repeated that he did 'not intend to alter anything'.[17] His total fidelity to the brickwork, glass and ornamental iron work of a particular urban locality which is the setting for a human drama is perhaps above all else what gives the painting its Victorian feel. The glass and iron arches of Paddington Station, so accurately drawn in for Frith by Scott Morton, even the near brick wall and the far curve of Blackfriar's Bridge, the destined background for the fallen woman in Rossetti's unfinished *Found,* are merely variations on and expansions of Wilkie's *Chelsea.* Following his habitual practice Wilkie worked from living models, selected in this instance from actual Pensioners, but he also utilised a device that he had only tried out once before, a device that enabled him to light his drama with accuracy and consistency, and to invest it with a more forceful three-dimensional and tactile realism than his other pictures had possessed. This device, adopted from Venetian and Dutch precedent, was a box containing clay models of all the figures 'properly coloured and put in a proper light and shaddow [*sic*]' one of 'the most powerful helps next to nature itself for determining the effect of a picture'.[18]

The extraordinary realism, patriotic subject, and high price of 1200 guineas 'greater' Wilkie admitted 'than . . . any other modern artists have had from any individual employer in this country'[19] led to such pressure to see the painting at the Royal Academy that a crash barrier had to be erected in front for its preservation. This barrier—another unique first—

51. Frith celebrates the diversity of society and the excitement of modern technology in *The railway station,* a view of Paddington (*cat.45*)

seems to have obsessed Frith as a record to be emulated. For the young aspirant artists of Frith's generation Wilkie was a venerated figure. To be addressed by him was an affair for recollection in one's autobiography, to have one's picture approved by him was a profound honour. 'Your friends expect you to be a second Wilkie' the art master Sass threw at Frith in a moment of extreme irritation, 'I can't make Wilkies and if I could, I should not make the experiment out of such material as you'.[20] Not surprisingly when Frith achieved his own barrier in front of his *Derby Day* at the R.A. exhibition of 1858 it was with a jubilant consciousness of having at last caught up with his dead hero. More than *Ramsgate Sands,* or even *Derby Day,* Frith's *Railway Station* is a work in the manner of the *Chelsea Pensioners.* It does not imitate the individual arrangement and grouping of Wilkie's picture, widely familiar though it was through the engraving, and from Denning's copy belonging to Frederick Goodall's father, but adapts the idea to a new set of circumstances. Goodall, who as a boy 'never wearied' of looking at Denning's copy, attributed to this the circumstance of his taking up the painting of English domestic life,[21] and the *Pensioners* seems to have operated with similar effect upon Frith, though with him it was Wilkie's conception of modernity and the passing moment that was of most interest. Frith's railway station epitomises urban modernity, and the departure of the train pins the moment chosen to one particular second in the mid-nineteenth century. The train is real, the station one we know. The people too seem convincingly real and individual. But as with *The Chelsea Pensioners,* it is only when we come to consider the range of situations presented, involving family life, schooling, young love, marriage, old age, crime and detection, foreigners, the army, the navy and press, that we realise the trick that is being played. 'All human life is here' and the seeming unique event masks the universal type.

52. Wilkie's friend Mulready began his *Convalescent from Waterloo* the year *The Chelsea Pensioners* was exhibited (*cat.44*)

Wilkie's friend Mulready, responded to the *Pensioners* in a very different manner with his *Convalescent* or *Convalescent from Waterloo* (*cat.44*), begun in 1822, the year *The Chelsea Pensioners* was exhibited, but not sold until 1826. Only knowledge of Mulready's belligerent character and passion for pugilism can save the modern viewer from mis-interpreting this apparently somewhat melancholy scene as an indictment of war—the wounded veteran father, the quarrelling children, aggression persisting from one generation to another! Mulready in fact approved of aggression. He took Wilkie's suggestion that modern patriotism and national victories do not have to be displayed by views of generals on battlefields, but can be explored equally effectively via the aftermath within family relationships—husband, wife, parent, child—but his subject, as usual, has an ambiguity for the interpreter that Wilkie's lacks.

The Chelsea Pensioners was exhibited in Scotland in 1837, reluctantly promised, crated, and dispatched across the January seas by the Duke of Wellington,[22] but whatever subtle influence upon Scottish artists it may have exercised, it prompted them to no such celebrations of urban modernity as Frith's *Railway Station*. Scotland indeed scarcely had any painting— outside portraiture—explicitly devoted to modern life. Her top artists of the 1840s and 50s, Drummond, Fettes Douglas, and Noel Paton, were by nature antiquarians with their faces turned back towards the past. We have seen how the interpretation of national identity and language as products of the past and of a tradition that were actually endangered by modern progress could make this antiquarianism easy for the artist, and Wilkie, at the very point of completing *The Chelsea Pensioners* was beginning what was for him an entirely new kind of picture, a historical reconstruction of the events which had led to the Scottish religious Reformation. It was by this, rather than *The Chelsea Pensioners,* that he was to make his mark on his own countrymen.

NOTES : MODERN LIFE

1. Cunningham, vol.1, p.105.

2. 'Orrock, in his occupation of blacksmith, was employed to manufacture some of the arms . . . These were pikes, and a sort of Lochaber axe . . . Questioned by visitors what these strange looking articles were, he was wont to say that they were ornaments for a gentleman's gate.' Cumberland Hill, *Historic Memorials and Reminiscences of Stockbridge* 2nd ed., Edinburgh 1887.

3. Alexander Bethune, in a letter of 31 July 1837, published in McCombie, *Memoirs of Alexander Bethune* Aberdeen 1845, p.127.

4. See A. R. B. Haldane, *Three centuries of Scottish posts* Edinburgh 1971, pp.164-70. Haldane also points out that the French war stimulated a demand for news and an increase in newspapers.

5. *Life of Benjamin Robert Haydon* ed. Tom Taylor, 3 vols, 2nd ed., London 1853, vol.2, pp.317-23 and 367.

6. Professor Wilson, *Noctes Ambrosianae* (originally contributed to *Blackwood's Magazine* 1822-35), a new edition in 4 vols, Edinburgh and London 1863, vol.2, December 1829, pp.290-91.

7. I am grateful to John Pinkerton for providing me with copious information on the Scottish and English bankruptcy laws and especially on the reform of the latter in 1813.

8. *Letters of Sir Charles Bell selected from his correspondence with his brother* London 1870, letter of 16 May 1814.

9. *Memoirs and recollections of the late Abraham Raimbach* ed. M. T. S. Raimbach, London 1843, pp.163-64.

10. *Life of Benjamin Robert Haydon* ed. Tom Taylor, 3 vols, 2nd edition, London 1853, vol.1, p.308.

11. *Autobiographical recollections of Charles Leslie* ed. Tom Taylor, 2 vols, London 1860, vol.1, p.215, and *Memoirs and Recollections of the late Abraham Raimbach* ed. M. T. S. Raimbach, London 1843, p.123.

12. A transcript of a letter by Wilkie, addressed to Clarkson Stanfield and dated January 1832, is pasted to the back of the panel of *Distraining,* and gives an account of the artist's reactions to the performance of Jerrold's drama, and its relationship with his painting.

13. *The P. R. B. Journal* ed. William E. Fredeman, Oxford 1975, p.60.

14. See Wilkie's catalogue description at the RA exhibition of 1822 (126).

15. Quoted in translation by Lorenz E. A. Eitner in *Géricault, his life and work* London 1983, p.218.

16. Letter from Wilkie to Perry Nursey, dated 24 July 1820, British Library, Department of Manuscripts, MS Additional 29,991.

17. Letter from Wilkie to Geddes dated 30 December 1821 quoted in David Laing, *Etchings by Sir David Wilkie, RA and by Andrew Geddes, ARA* Edinburgh 1875, p.14.

18. See note 16, op. cit.

19. Letter from Wilkie to Perry Nursey dated 28 July 1822, British Library, Department of Manuscripts, MS Additional 29,991.

20. W. P. Frith, *My autobiography and reminiscences* 2 vols, London 1887, vol.1, p.51.

21. *The reminiscences of Frederick Goodall* London and Newcastle-on-Tyne 1902, p.19.

22. MS letter from the Duke of Wellington dated from Stratfield Saye, 19 January 1837, RSA Library.

Religion, History and Travel

WILKIE'S already quoted notion that Scotland should be regarded as 'a volume of history' was expressed only three days after his return from his Scottish tour of 1817. He had come south straight from Abbotsford, where he had been painting the Scott family in a semi-genre grouping—'a sort of subject'—and wearing 'the dresses of the common people of the country',[1] the girls as the ewe milkers who figure so often in Scottish border songs and ballads, and Scott in Wilkie's words, 'as if telling a story'.[2] In the background were the Cowdenknowes, the Tweed and Melrose. It was as a teller of old tales that Wilkie regarded Scott, and so the borders, equally Scott's subject matter and his home thus became invested in Wilkie's eyes also with 'history', 'tradition' and 'poetry'. It was almost certainly under the influence of Scott's way of looking at his country that Wilkie turned to the painting of Scottish history in his *Knox preaching at St Andrews*. In the summer of 1822 when Wilkie went north to cover the visit to Edinburgh of George IV he carried with him the lively oil sketch (now at Petworth) expressly to show to Scott, who was much impressed by its power.[3] Unfortunately the breakdown in Wilkie's health and his subsequent Italian tour interrupted work on the large version which was not completed and exhibited until ten years later, in 1832. It is not surprising that the connection between the two men, Scott and Wilkie, was instantly spotted by Waagen when he saw the *Knox* in 1835. 'In this picture ... I fancied that I actually saw before me those fanatical Puritans whom Walter Scott so admirably describes, and was again convinced of the congeniality between him and Wilkie.'[4] To Waagen there was a twofold resemblance, consisting first in the intensity of feeling and the actuality of the realisation, secondly in the accuracy of the historical detail, so that the picture seemed at once immediate and yet remote in time. His experience was shared by Uwins who felt the conflict of contending emotions in the picture as 'terrific', and yet was at the same time able to stand back from the subject and estimate it as 'a complete history of the Reformation'.[5] This double aspect of the picture is something that must be considered in a little more detail.

At the time of Wilkie's visit to Abbotsford, he of course knew Scott as the Editor of the *Border Minstrelsy* and author of the narrative poems but he was uncertain about Scott's authorship of the novels. A year later he appears to have lost his doubts, and discussed Scott's 'projects' including *The Bride of Lammermoor* just as if there had been no incognito.[6] Wilkie was evidently reading the novels promptly, as they appeared, and he must have observed how Scott was gradually working further and further back into the past. *Rob Roy* of 1818 which Wilkie called 'a work of genius' had included a highly evocative description of a preaching in the dusky shadows of the Laigh Kirk at Glasgow, an episode compared by the author to the Raphael cartoon of Paul preaching at Athens. *Rob Roy* was set in the Scotland of the period immediately prior to the 1717 Rebellion. *Old Mortality* published 1816 had been set a little earlier, in the era of the Covenanters, towards the end of the seventeenth century. Both had dealt with religio-political conflicts. In *The Monastery* and *The Abbot,* published 1820, Scott moved himself back by yet another century into the middle of the Scottish Reformation. The following year Wilkie embarked upon his chalk drawing of *Knox preaching* (Fitzwilliam Museum). Scott's strength in his historical novels lay in his ability to invest the events of history with movement and excitement, to renew the now settled conflicts of principle as vital and uncertain questions and make the characters themselves come alive for the reader. Transformed by his powerful imagination, the material of his historical research re-emerged as gripping stories instead of dry dissertations. Wilkie too engaged in various kinds of research. His historical text was taken from M'Crie's *Life of John Knox* (1813), the same M'Crie who had so hotly disputed Scott's uncomplimentary portrait of the Covenanters. He investigated the appearance of Knox's pulpit. 'I am studding it all round with carvings in low and high relief of Saints, Apostles and Martyrs, with cheribine and cherophine supporting crowns over their heads. Perhaps some other specimens of this sort in the picture may be no bad indication of some of the labour which his preaching destroyed.'[7]—So ambivalent did Wilkie feel towards the Reformation after seeing the religious art of Italy! The atmosphere and colour of the historical moment Wilkie sought in Rubens' painting of the *Coronation of Marie de Medici* which he had admired on his visit to France. It was the nearest he could get to an authentic presentation of his chosen period without actually imitating the dry and flat painters who had really been Knox's contemporaries. In the final version of the subject when Wilkie was seek-

53. Wilkie's interpretation of the conflicts of the Scottish Reformation in
John Knox preaching

ing a more inward and reflective presentation of a new versus an old
religion he chose as a model Rembrandt's *Woman taken in Adultery*,[8] in
which the new Gospel of Christ is set against the vast shadowy edifice of
the ancient Jewish temple, at once black, mysterious and seductively
glittering. It is of some interest that Turner, at much the same moment
was apparently drawing on the effects of the same Rembrandt for his
Christ driving the Traders from the Temple, and *Pilate washing his hands*.[9]
It is highly possible that Turner knew exactly what Wilkie was doing with
Rembrandt in his *Knox*, and that he was once more publicly pitting himself
against Wilkie, this time with the object of showing that Rembrandt
should be interpreted as a painter of light rather than of darkness.

It would be a mistake however, as I have already suggested, to regard
the *Knox* as wholly committed to the past. That sermon at St Andrews had
worked a permanent change upon worship in Scotland, and the sermon
itself was still, in Wilkie's day, the hub of the Scottish service. He himself
was fascinated by preaching simply as a form of art, and by the technical
mastery which enabled the preacher to hold his congregation. (In this
respect the *Knox* follows *The Blind Fiddler*.) In a letter written to his
friend Nursey, while Wilkie was working on the *Knox*, he emphasises that
the preacher must 'have his own attention alive and on the alert for
between that and the attention of his congregation there must be a per-

6. David Wilkie, *Chelsea Pensioners receiving the London Gazette
Extraordinary announcing the Battle of Waterloo* (cat.38 detail)

7. William Powell Frith, *The railway station* (cat.45 detail)
8. Robert Braithwaite Martineau, *Last day in the old home* (cat.43)

petual sympathy'.[10] He was at that time taking a marked interest in the preaching of two very different men, both of whom were his personal friends.

The first of these was Thomas Chalmers, at that time minister of St John's Church, Glasgow. Wilkie drew him preaching on at least two occasions, both probably prior to November 1823 when he preached his last sermon in the ministry before taking a professor's chair. Chalmers though a distinguished man, and one who ultimately became the leader in the great walk-out from the Assembly of the Scottish Church which signalised the Disruption, did not look distinguished. He seems to have possessed a chubby face and cropped hair with a tendency to stick up in tufts. It is not feasible that Wilkie looked to Chalmers in any way as the physical model for his Knox preaching, 'like an Eagle swooping over his prey' as one contemporary aptly described him. The case is otherwise when one turns to Wilkie's other chosen preacher, Edward Irving. Irving, a giant of charismatic presence, and long greasy black hair, with a weird, antiquated style of delivery modelled upon Scottish divines of the sixteenth and seventeenth centuries, was a figure of exotic power who looked like an Italian assassin and was once mistaken for Paganini, the demoniac violinist. From his induction on the second sabbath of July 1822 (that is at the very point of time when Wilkie at the Earl of Liverpool's request began his oil sketch for *Knox*), Irving was electrifying his listeners at the Caledonian Chapel, Hatton Garden, causing queues, traffic jams, and fainting and tears amongst his congregation. Irving had first come to London on Christmas Eve 1821. He then returned to Scotland and did not come south until just before his induction which was attended by Chalmers. He bore a letter of introduction to Wilkie who became a regular attender at the Chapel. Chalmers for instance described meeting him in the vestry, with Thomas Lawrence after a service in September 1822 and a year later we find Wilkie concerned about newspaper attacks on Irving.[11] Burnet reports him as comparing Irving to Paul preaching at Athens[12] (again, probably it was Raphael's cartoon that was meant). A contemporary pen and ink sketch of Irving preaching (by James Atkinson)[13] shows features very similar to those of Wilkie's *Knox,* a prominent aquiline nose, a pronounced forehead and chin, and long straight hair. It would be a mistake to regard Wilkie's historical subject as only a disguised piece of contemporary life. It was surely intended for a recreation, as truthful as Wilkie could make it, of the historical Knox in action, but of a Knox and his impact made real and immediate for the painter by his first hand experience of Irving's power over his congregation at the Caledonian Chapel, and it is typical of Wilkie's alertness to the things of importance happening round him that he chose to recreate Knox via the personalities of two nineteenth-century preachers, both of whom were later to become leaders of schisms from the established Kirk.

Wilkie's *Knox* had a marked effect on the work of at least three Scottish artists. The first of these was his friend William Allan, who must

54. Sixteenth-century passion and violence interpreted by William Allan in *The death of Rizzio,* painted after a visit with Wilkie to Queen Mary's apartments in Holyrood (*cat.55*)

have seen the oil sketch which Wilkie brought to Edinburgh in 1822. Hitherto Allan's subjects had mainly been concerned with the adventurous lives of Tartars, Circassians and Russian peasants. In 1819, however, he painted a scene from Scott's novel *The Heart of Midlothian,* and in 1823, the year after seeing the sketch for *Knox* he exhibited his own scene from the Reformer's life, *Knox admonishing Mary Queen of Scots,* and followed this up in 1824 with *Lord Lindsay compelling Mary to abdicate* (an episode described by Scott in *The Abbot*). Whilst it might be going too far to claim that these were executed under Wilkie's supervision, they were almost certainly produced in close consultation with him, and a letter of 4 April 1824 from Wilkie to Allan, contains a lengthy, detailed critique of the abdication picture and especially of its 'light and shaddow'.[14] Wilkie and Allan visited Holyrood House together in 1817, lingering in the apartment where Rizzio was murdered,[15] and their joint visit provided Allan with yet another subject from Mary's life, which he began to paint, under a renewed impetus from Wilkie's ideas, in the year 1832 when the finished *Knox preaching* was finally exhibited. 'I . . . have been very busy with the subject I mentioned to you, the murder of David Rizzio' (*cat.55*), he wrote to Wilkie in October that year, 'I am well on with it and I hope to have it finished in good time for next exhibition',[16] and exhibited indeed it was at the R.A. of 1833. Its colour range, and the deep bituminous shadows out of which violent events erupt, with torchlight flashing on anguished faces, on metal arms, silks and velvets, are all so like Wilkie's *Knox* that together they seem to constitute the beginning of a national school of historical painting. Yet Allan's *Rizzio* is after all pure romance and glamour. Physically it resembles Wilkie's work, but intellectually it misses the extra

55. A novel combination of genre and history painting derived from two phases of Wilkie's career. George Harvey's *Covenanters' preaching* (cat.54)

dimension that Wilkie shared with Scott, the conviction that incompatible principles of permanent relevance underlie such historical conflicts. Where Wilkie shows the confrontation of these principles, with the violence they will unleash, Allan shows us love, jealousy and private murder.

Glamour is hardly the word to be applied to Wilkie's second Scottish follower George Harvey, who recreated history in the language of the *Village Politicians* rather than of *Knox and the Lords of the Congregation.* Low life as history was a new idea which Harvey seems to have reached by the expedient of amalgamating Wilkie's early genre style and characters with the later historical subjects. He became a specialist in covenanting themes.

The third artist to fall under Wilkie's spell was Thomas Duncan. Duncan's work was closer in spirit to that of Allan whose pupil he had been, than to that of Harvey. He too turned frequently to Scott for subjects to illustrate, but his most important historical picture *Prince Charles Edward and the Highlanders entering Edinburgh after the Battle of Prestonpans* (1841) is not taken from Scott. The *Prince Charles* draws on two of Wilkie's contemporary subjects, *Chelsea Pensioners* and the *Entry of George IV into Holyrood,* and one historical subject, *Knox preaching.* Its indebtedness to these three pictures is revealed, not only in the design, but in an odd fact about it. Duncan's catalogue entry, when it was exhibited at the R.A., is exactly like the type of extended catalogue entry with biographical information on each of the main figures, which Wilkie had begun to use at the time of the *Chelsea Pensioners* and continued for *George IV* and *Knox.*

One of the least satisfactory of Wilkie's legacies to his successors was a technical method which called for liberal amounts of the attractive but unstable asphaltum, which never fully dries out, but tends to change from a translucent glowing brown to something as opaque and dirty as the

56. The great and the lesser attend one of the first Protestant Sacraments. Sketch for *Knox dispensing the Sacrament,* Wilkie's sequel to *Knox preaching (cat.49)*

surface of a tar macadamed road. The use of asphaltum (the most 'gorgeous' of colours according to Wilkie)[17] is the distinguishing mark separating the school of historical painting founded by Wilkie, and based on oil painting techniques, from the school of historical painting influenced by Nazarene and German example, and based on mural painting techniques. Both the material substances employed by Wilkie's followers and the dark tonality of their visual effects were totally unsuited to direct application on the surface of walls. Since historical painting in the mid-nineteenth century flourished chiefly in connection with the decoration of the Houses of Parliament and other public buildings, the Wilkie style was ousted by the revivalist Germanic styles, psychologically naive and old-fashioned but technically far more suited to architecture.

Although most of Wilkie's followers in the dark historical style were Scotsmen working in Scotland, there are odd outcrops in the South as well. *The Trial of Charles I* (Fyvie collection) was bought as a Wilkie, but has been reattributed to Burnet by the Irwins,[18] and is almost slavishly based on *Knox preaching.* Burnet, of course, was a Scot, but Windus, who is more generally known as a nervous and over-sensitive Pre-Raphaelite, at an earlier stage in his career produced an illustration to Scott's *Old Mortality, Morton before Claverhouse at Tillietudlem (cat.56)* in which the combination of Scott's historical writing with the subject of conflict between the rival religious beliefs of Royalists and Covenanters, seems to have acted as a cue to an oil sketch in the free style of *Knox preaching.*

When Wilkie began his second Reformation scene, the composition of *Knox dispensing the Sacrament* (*cat.49*) he was thinking less in terms of the dramatic reconstruction of past events, as in a Scott novel, and more in terms of the devotional pictures he had seen in Catholic Italy and Spain. Commenting, in 1839, upon the Oxford Movement he wrote, 'Zeal is indispensible to uphold the Establishment, this zeal must be either High Church or Low Church, that is towards Catholic or evangelical doctrine. If to Catholic, they must call in Art, an auxiliary that Protestants have neglected, though even now Pictures might help the devotion of the former (probably a mistake for latter) class of people.'[19] The layout of his design, deliberately modelled upon Leonardo's *Last Supper,* emphasises the sacramental as opposed the narrative aspect of the event, and reminds the viewer that Knox is commemorating or repeating the primary actions of Jesus. Wilkie had again sought his subject in M'Crie's *Life of John Knox.* 'After his return to the south of the Forth, he resided at Calder House, in West Lothian, with Sir James Sandilands, commonly called Lord St John, because he was chief in Scotland of the religious order of military knights who went by the name of Hospitallers or Knights of St John. This knight who was now venerable for his grey hairs as well as for his valour, sagacity, and sobriety, had long been a sincere friend to the reformed cause.'

Wilkie planned to paint Sir James in armour as an indication of his military background. Knox's likeness seems to have been based on an old portrait of Knox which then hung at Calder House, and from which M'Crie had taken the engraved frontispiece of his book. The preparatory drawings indicate Wilkie's proposed background, but the hall of Calder now bears no resemblance—and in fact probably bore none in Wilkie's day either—to the architectural background he sketched out at the rear of Knox and the table. Wilkie seems to have already begun thinking about the Calder subject in 1837. In June 1838 he wrote to Sir William Knighton, 'The print of Knox is out and thought successful. A companion is called for for which Knox and the Sacrament now occupies my thoughts.'[20] This intended sequel was publicly announced 'as a warning to interlopers', but to no avail. Wilkie did not move fast enough, and in March 1840 we find him writing to Peel, 'I shall be glad to show you a beginning of a picture Mr Moon has given me a commission to paint for him which he is immediately to engrave, as the companion to John Knox preaching, being indeed urged to this by the circumstance of an Edinburgh artist being engaged by one of his rival London publishers, to paint a picture for the same purpose, and almost of the same subject that I was known to have selected.'[21] This story throws a fascinating sidelight upon the competitiveness of the early nineteenth-century engraving industry, indicating not only how large the expected financial rewards might be for a successful print, but also how vital originality of subject was for the achieving of this financial success.

Wilkie's letter also raises the intriguing question, who was his unnamed rival? To this question there are two or three possible answers but no real evidence that any of them are correct. Thomas Duncan died in 1845

57. Under the influence of Wilkie, James Drummond painted *George Wishart administering the Sacrament for the first time in the Protestant form* (*cat.59*)

leaving behind him an unfinished sketch for a large historical picture which he had been preparing 'some time' before his death to paint of *George Wishart dispensing the Sacrament in the Prison of the Castle of St Andrews 1546*. If this unfinished sketch was really commissioned by a rival to Moon then that publisher was probably Alexander Hill, brother of the artist D.O.Hill, who owned others of Duncan's works and who as Moon's agent in Scotland for the distribution of engravings after *Knox preaching*[22] might well have planned to annexe the market for an engraving of the first Protestant sacrament. Against this it has to be said that Wilkie's letter does seem to imply that Knox rather than Wishart was to be the hero of his rival's picture, and that the publisher was a London man. The Wishart subject, the first Protestant sacrament, was also painted in 1845 by James Drummond (*cat.59*), and the dependancy that both he and Duncan displayed on Wilkie's Knox prototype is probably very simply explained by the fact that that picture was now in Scotland, having been acquired by the R.S.A. in 1842. Once here it was to provide a lively and continuing influence upon Scottish art. D.O.Hill, for instance, who sketched it, and drew up the key to the identity of the figures when it first arrived,[23] also used it as the foundation for the composition of his painting of the *Disruption*.

A more surprising, and yet a more plausible candidate for the role of Wilkie's rival, than either Duncan or Drummond, is William Dyce. Dyce's undated *John Knox dispensing the Sacrament at Calder House* (*cat.58*) was in his sale after his death. It is hypothetically dated by Dr Pointon to 1835–7,[24] and is so very like Wilkie's oil sketch for the Knox that it is inconceivable that Dyce could have arrived at his own design without seeing the Wilkie, but it is noticeably much less like the final version of

58. William Dyce imitates Wilkie's style and presentation in his own version of *John Knox administering the Sacrament (cat.58)*

Wilkie's *Knox*. The odd thing about this picture is that Dyce, who took his religion very seriously as he did the religious function of art, was a high episcopalian. A Protestant sacrament dispensed by Knox would have been so little to his taste that he could never have selected it to please himself. The only plausible explanation for his painting this subject at all is that it was a commission, but if it was a commission then why, one asks, was it still on his hands some twenty-seven years later? The answer to this is provided, if the commission in due course fell through, perhaps because it appeared that Wilkie was buckling down to finish his own *Knox Sacrament* after all. Dyce came to London from Edinburgh in 1837, and is very likely as a Scot to have gained access to Wilkie's studio and seen the oil sketch which Wilkie produced for the *Knox at Calder*. This would put a hypothetical date of 1838 or 9 onto Dyce's own painting, for towards the end of 1839 the first intimation of the rival publisher's activity seems to have reached Wilkie's ear.

If this hypothesis is true it throws a slightly unpleasant light on Dyce's character, but true or not, the internal evidences of style and design prove him to have been working under Wilkie's influence, and we are faced with a choice between some kind of voluntary artistic espionage on Dyce's part, or an involuntary submission to an influence so compelling that it was able to counteract the bias of his own taste in art and beliefs in religion.

Between beginning *Knox preaching* and the commencement of its sequel, Wilkie had spent several years travelling on the continent. The character of ethnographical recorders, which was to some extent forced upon those Scottish Artists who came south to compete in London, may

59. The ancient ritual of the Roman Catholic church attracted Wilkie as
a subject when he visited Italy. Here *Cardinals, Priests and Roman
Citizens wash the Pilgrims' feet* (cat.48)

partly have contributed to the extensive journeys they made. In due
course, as the pictorial supply of the customs, scenery and architecture of
their own country became exhausted—or perhaps rather because they
feared the interest of a fickle public in these topics was becoming exhausted
—they were forced to travel. It was not accident or natural wanderlust that
drove Wilkie, William Allan, David Roberts and John Phillip to Italy,
Spain and the Middle East, so much as the necessity of perpetually introducing novelty into their subjects, anticipating market taste, and fore-
stalling the moves of rival artists.

   In painting Scotland they were dealing with what they knew inside
out. Abroad they were strangers seeing only the outside, and estimating
its interest or importance largely in terms of its difference from home
conditions. Two factors seem to have decided Wilkie's choice and treatment of foreign subjects. The first factor was his own search for the custom
or mode of behaviour that best encapsulated the essential nature of the
country and people he was studying. The second factor led out from the
first. Clearly Wilkie brought his own ideas on the nature of Italy, Spain
and Ireland with him, tending to find what he was already looking for, and
equally clearly, his public at home also possessed their own preformed

60. William Simson's *Camaldolese monk showing the
relics in the sacristy of a Roman Convent* (*cat.62*)

notions about foreign countries. He had therefore to characterise these
countries in terms of what was expected, pinpointing the exact aspects of
their cultures that also characterised the areas of his public's interest in
them.

Apart from scenery and architecture which were only ever marginal
elements in Wilkie's painting, the dress, behaviour and above all the
religion, the politics, and the history of its people are the most obvious
clues to a country's identity. In Italy, and more particularly in Rome—the
religious centre of the Catholic world—the overwhelming power of the
Church, the age and pictorial appeal of its rituals, and its long relationship
with the arts, decided the question of Wilkie's subjects for him. He arrived
in the Holy Year, and the ceremonies of Holy Week with the conjunction
between the simplicity of the pilgrim peasants and the pomp of the high
dignitaries of the church humbled in acts of public penance, fascinated him
(*cat.48*).

The painter Uwins, who seems to have been a rigid, literal-minded
and somewhat naive Protestant, was in Rome at the same period, appalled
by the superstitions, shocked by the rituals, and gloating over the paucity
of pilgrims and the fact that the Holy Year as a public function seemed
likely to prove a spectacular failure for the Pope.[25] Wilkie's approach was
infinitely more sensitive, and was also that of a more balanced and widely
cultured mind. He refused to be drawn on simply issues of right or wrong,

true or false. Instead one senses his attempt to connect, by means of colour, draughtsmanship, and compositional arrangement, the present rituals of confession and penance he was observing, with works by the artists in the past service of the Catholic Church, Raphael and Michelangelo, whose frescoes in chapel and Stanze he was also studying in detail. A new set of greys and lavenders appeared in his painting, and forms were broadened and simplified. Internally he was relating all he observed to his own meditations on the history of religion and the role of the artist in relation to the church. His Holy Week subjects and his treatment of them were later closely followed by the Scottish artist Simson who was in Italy in 1836 (*cat.62*).

Moving on to Spain in 1827, Wilkie rejected overtly religious subjects in favour of political and military ones. His priests and peasants collaborate in guerilla warfare. His Spanish heroine Augustina does not kneel to wash and kiss the dirty feet of pilgrims but fires a cannon against the French.[26] Here the operation of market considerations must have been paramount in Wilkie's mind. The most recent British connection with Spain was that of the Peninsular war and Wellington's campaign. Behind that lay an image of a country full of wild and picaresque characters such as are described in Smollet's popular translation of Le Sage's *Gil Blas*. Wilkie gave united visible form to both associations, looking, inventing, and combining, as he had done in Italy, merging first-hand observation with suggestions from the historical work of Murillo and Velasquez. So powerful was his mélange that Lewis and John ('Spanish') Phillip who followed him to Spain seem to have drawn on it as if it were a visual guidebook to the artist in Spain.

In Ireland in 1835 Wilkie rediscovered the Catholicity of Italy and Spain, along with the primitive wildness of the latter country, suggesting to him that modern civilization had slid by, leaving it halted in a state of untouched prehistory, a fragile living link with the past. How far he was correct in his view cannot be discussed here, but it was precisely the same belief that he took with him to Syria, and on a realisation of which the entire success of his religious art work there depended—a conviction that though some cultures move fast some are static, and that the static ones can therefore provide the clue to what life was really like in remote periods. Travel to Wilkie was thus also a method of historical delving.

Again and again in his letters from Ireland his descriptions of the way of life in Galway and Connemara reiterate this theme. 'A state of primeval simplicity', 'an age of poetry', 'most simple and pastoral conditions' are some of the phrases used. 'The clothes particularly of the women are the work of their own hands and the colour they are most fond of is a red they dye with madder . . . Indeed the whole economy of the people furnishes the elements of the picturesque. They build their own cabins, fabricate their own clothes, dig their own turf, catch their own salmon and plough their own fields bringing into their dwelling a confused variety of impliments [*sic*] not to be described.'[27] Although in the *Peep o' day boy's Cabin* and

61. The primitive aspects of Irish life were what attracted Wilkie.
The Irish Whiskey Still of 1840 (*cat.47*)

the *Irish Whiskey Still* (*cat.47*) Wilkie purports to be covering modern political and social problems, these titles are merely camouflage. 'When Adam delved and Eve span' seems nearer the mark. He was terrified that some other painter might nip in and manage to exploit this goldmine before him.

Wilkie's anticipation of potential rivalry was correct in that he was followed to Ireland much as he was followed to Spain by a succession of later artists, keen to work the new vein of ore he had opened. Goodall (who later also followed him to the Middle East) was one. Another was the Scot, Erskine Nicol. Nicol's primitivism is not of the high and romantic order envisaged by Wilkie. His Irish are not primal heroes but rustic clowns. They are the village politicians transported westward, and their consumption of illicit spirit only leads to fights and sore heads as we see in *The day after the fair* (*cat.61*).

Nicol is copious with the kind of detail we are given in early Wilkie pictures, the detail that points to the present moment. Only by comparing his presentation of the Irish cabin with Wilkie's can we fully appreciate Wilkie's reserve and discretion over such detail. Timelessness not modernity was now his object, and so we have the madder petticoats reminiscent as he thought of Titian and Giorgione, the naked putti of Correggio, the satanic apparatus of the still, but not the bonnets, shawls and teapots of the nineteenth century. All in all Wilkie's trip to Ireland seems a suitable mental preliminary to his last journey to the East.

62. Erskine Nicol's *Day after the fair* turns Wilkie's noble Irish savages into comedians (*cat.61*)

Scott, whose *Talisman* of 1825, is set amongst the Crusaders fighting for the possession of Jerusalem, admitted in his *Introduction* of 1832 the difficulty he had found in providing a 'vivid' portrait of a Palestine which he had never visited but which had recently been described and visited by so many British travellers. Amongst the gathering crowd of travellers to the East were artists. Finden's *Landscape Illustrations of the Bible* published 1835–36 included thirty plates by Turner based on drawings by other artists. David Roberts was in Egypt and Syria in 1838. His water-colours, later published as sets of chromo-lithographs, *Views in the Holy Land, Syria, Idumea, Arabia Egypt and Nubia,* were exhibited on his return to London. Roberts had visited Spain after Wilkie, acting on Wilkie's advice, but he preceded his friend to the Holy Land. Roberts' interests were, however, primarily scenic and architectural, whereas William Allan, whose *Slave Market, Constantinople* of 1838 was the fruit of a visit to Greece and Asia Minor some eight or nine years earlier, had similar tastes to Wilkie. His subject is neither landscape nor architecture, but the physical and cultural characteristics of the different races of the East, Arab, Turk, Negro and Circassian. Each of these is provided with his or her appropriate dress, and Allan was careful to record typical social customs as in the squatting figures sharing a hookah in the foreground.

Between this search for exotic ethnographic information, this gradual accumulation in Britain during the 1830s of visual records of the cities, ruins, deserts and races of the East, and a painting such as Holman Hunt's *Finding of the Saviour in the Temple,* there was a gap to be bridged, its nature pin-pointed by the conversation Disraeli imagined as taking place in his novel *Tancred* (1847) at Bethany, between his English hero and

63. Wilkie's *Turkish letter writer* shows a Greek and a Turkish girl in an
incident glimpsed in Constantinople (*cat.52*)

Jewish heroine. 'Ah! the mother of Jesus!' said his companion, 'He is your
God. He lived much in this village. He was a great man, but he was a Jew;
and you worship him . . . he was born a Jew, lived a Jew, and died a Jew, as
became a Prince of the House of David, which you do and must acknowledge him to have been. Your sacred genealogies prove the fact.' This gap
between the busy accumulation of records on Eastern architecture and
landscape—Holy Places—and the admission that Jesus and the Disciples
—the Holy persons—had been in fact Jews, in custom and dress probably

64. John Lewis' *Arab scribe, Cairo* is based on Wilkie's design (*cat.63*)

bearing a recognisable resemblance to their nineteenth-century Palestinian descendants, was first bridged for painting by Wilkie.

It seems inevitable that his ever widening travels into remote territories should eventually have carried him to the Holy Land, where his deepening interest in the religious functions of art, and his taste for tracing ancient and primitive habits continued in the folk customs and dresses still extant in the nineteenth century, were combined into the idea of a new religious painting, or more strictly speaking, the re-animation and correction of the older models of Christian art by the incorporation of accurately observed or reconstructed facts about Oriental location, race, dress and custom. The desire to correct and purify Christian art by the science of accurate observation and historical research is analogous to and yet utterly different from the purification of religious art that had been attempted by the Nazarenes whose work Wilkie had encountered and had criticised, in Rome. The Nazarenes had effected their purge by pushing art back to that approximate date in the fifteenth century when it seemed at its purest and most spiritual as an expression of innocent faith. To Wilkie, as a Protestant, desiring to experience and think matters out for himself, and as an artist, devoted to exploiting the mysterious powers of atmospheric colour and chiaroscuro, it could never have been satisfactory to halt belief and knowledge in the late Middle Ages, or stop painting at the moment before chiaroscuro was invented. The clearest statement of his purpose—an oddly humble purpose—is contained in a letter that he wrote

65. An unfinished study of *Jewish groups in a synagogue* (possibly on
Mount Zion) sketched by Wilkie at Jerusalem in 1841

to Sir Robert Peel, in 1841, from Jerusalem. 'It is a fancy as belief that the
art of our time, and of our British people may require it, that has indiced
me to undertake this journey. It is to see, to enquire, and to judge, not
whether I can, but whether those who are younger and with far higher
attainments and power, may not in future be required, in the advance and
spread of our knowledge to refer at once to the localities of Scripture
events, when the great work is to be essayed of representing Scripture
History . . . It is remarkable that none of the great painters to whom the
world has hitherto looked for the visible appearance of Scripture Scenes
and feelings have ever visited the Holy Land.'[28] He pointed out that the
Venetians (the inventors of atmospheric colour) through their Levantine
contacts had been enabled to give their inventions a nearer 'verisimilitude
to an Eastern people', and wondered what effect working in the East would
have had on Raphael and Leonardo (inventors of modern chiaroscuro). He
talked of the people to be seen in Jerusalem 'The Jew, the Arab,—and the
more humble and destitute, who never change—recall, by their appearance a period of antiquity in every way removed from the present time',
and he concluded that 'To the expounder of Scripture, and to the painter of
sacred history, this whole territory must supply what can be learnt no
where else.' It is not by chance that Wilkie in this letter home refers to the

66. The features of the *Persian prince, Halicoo Mirza,*
whose slave offers him refreshment, were later used
by Wilkie as models for the head of Christ (*cat.51*)

Venetians, Leonardo, Raphael, and elsewhere to Rembrandt, as artists
who were actually slightly affected by existing Jewish or Levantine contacts, or who would have benefited by a journey similar to his own. He saw
these artists as his precursors, modern in their investigation into the
truth, their reliance on first hand visual experience.

Whilst he was in the East, Wilkie produced various types of picture.
He painted several formal portraits with which we are not concerned here.
He made a number of vividly coloured highly finished studies of single
figures or groups in elaborate and beautiful costumes. Usually in these
some action is involved—the *Muleteer* (*cat.53*) for instance is praying—so
that the figures verge on genre rather than portrait. He made some studies
of characteristic episodes—Jews reading in a Synagogue, Jews at the
Wailing Wall for example—and, lastly, he began a small number of
imagined oil studies, illustrations to the *Gospels—The Nativity, Christ
before Pilate* and *The Supper at Emmaus.* His sudden death on the return
voyage left these projects as it left *Knox dispensing the Sacrament* (*cat.50*),

9. David Wilkie, *Unfinished painting of John Knox dispensing the Sacrament at Calder House* (*cat.50* detail)

10. David Wilkie, *A Persian Prince, his slave bringing him sherbet*
(*cat.51*)

67. Apostles in oriental costume, a detail from Lauder's *Christ teacheth
humility* of 1847, influenced by Wilkie's example

in an unfinished state, and for thirteen years no one else took up the
challenging, expensive, and uncertain task of authentic scriptural illustration. It is true that Robert Scott Lauder, drawing on the experiences and
costumes acquired in the East by his friend David Roberts, produced, in his
large Westminster Hall competition picture, *Christ Teacheth Humility,*
some convincingly Arabian garbed Apostles and Disciples, but he had not
visited the Holy Land himself and his work is a compromise, a curtsy in the
direction of modern knowledge and travel experience, rather than an
expression of burning personal commitment.

Holman Hunt, who in 1854 took up the gauntlet left by Wilkie, had
been familiar, from his earliest student days, when he had copied *The
Blind Fiddler* in the British Museum, with his predecessor's work. His
references, in his book *Pre Raphaelitism,* to Wilkie are a series of strange
contradictions, and his comments on Wilkie's Eastern studies—we do not
know which he had actually seen—are disparaging. It is difficult to avoid
suspecting that his belittlement of Wilkie's undertaking arose partly from
a wish, in his old age, to stress his own originality.

Hunt was more dogged in the pursuit of factual historical minutiae
than Wilkie. He was also more interested in landscape and more concerned
about symbolism than his precursor. *The Scapegoat* is a subject that would
never even have occurred to Wilkie as worth painting. *The finding of
Christ in the Temple,* on the other hand, with its semi-circle of learned
rabbis of varying ages and characters, squatting oriental fashion on the
ground, about the figure of the boy Jesus, is closer to the situations which
interested Wilkie, and for which he was hunting out material. The question whether Jesus and his followers would have sat on chairs or on the
ground was indeed the very one which Wilkie had debated with friends in
Jerusalem. A living bridge between the art of Hunt and the art of Wilkie,

68. This detail of rabbis' heads from Holman Hunt's *Finding of the Saviour in the Temple* shows the final use to which Hunt put his researches amongst the synagogues in Jerusalem

from the ethnographic and stylistic—if not from the religious—viewpoints, was provided by the watercolourist John Lewis who had been in the East at the same time as Wilkie and whom Hunt met in 1851 after Lewis's return from his long sojourn in Cairo. Lewis had been in contact with Wilkie at Constantinople in 1840, and just as his earlier Spanish watercolours had reflected Wilkie's treatment of such themes, so too the scale and style of his early oriental figure scenes closely echoed the methods and attitudes of Wilkie. In due course Lewis' style moved naturally further from that of Wilkie towards a colouristic brilliance and elaboration of detail that prefigures Pre-Raphaelitism, but even in some of the later pictures he was still content to play variations on original themes by Wilkie (*cat.63*).

69. Wilkie's unfinished *Knox dispensing the Sacrament* reveals the proto-Pre-Raphaelite method of painting which later influenced Holman Hunt (*cat.50*)

The brilliance and clarity of colour in some of Wilkie's oriental studies, though not of a Pre-Raphaelite intensity, is nevertheless far higher in key than one would expect from the painter of *Knox preaching* or *The Irish Whiskey Still,* or indeed from any artist with such strong views as Wilkie held on the degenerate modern tendency to paint in a light tonality. Both Holman Hunt and Wilkie were artists who believed passionately that there were right and wrong ways of painting pictures, and their respective attitudes appear on the face of it so much at variance, that it may seem perverse to attempt to establish any connection between them, even via the agency of John Lewis. Nevertheless we know, because Hunt felt it worth recording, that whilst copying *The Blind Fiddler* as a student, he received a most important account of the method by which it had been painted from Claude Lorraine Nursey the son of Wilkie's friend Perry Nursey. 'Wilkie painted it without any dead colouring (i.e. matt under painting), finishing each bit thoroughly in a day . . . he had been Wilkie's

70. Rossetti's unfinished *Found* shows the painting method learnt from Hunt and partly derived from Wilkie. Detailed portions completed separately, on a white ground (*cat.65*)

pupil, and had been taught his then singular practice.'[29] Claude Lorraine Nursey could not of course have possessed any personal recollection of the execution of *The Blind Fiddler*. He must have been relying on Wilkie's later painting method and on what Wilkie himself told him. Nursey's information is however borne out by what Burnet says of the lack of dead colouring in *The Fiddler* and its completion, piece by piece, across the surface.[30] Much of the clarity and brilliance of Pre-Raphaelite pictures is due to the white ground on which they were painted and the completion of each portion at a sitting. True, *The Blind Fiddler* does not look in the least like a Pre-Raphaelite picture, but Wilkie's last major work, the *Knox dispensing the Sacrament,* with its finely detailed heads and jewel-like colours harshly contrasted to the acreage of blank white priming surrounding them, has a recognisable technical, and even stylistic affinity with Rossetti's unfinished *Found*—the most Hunt-like painting by a Pre-

Raphaelite artist who had been, if briefly, Hunt's pupil. Only fourteen years separate the execution of these two pictures.

Was Wilkie, it becomes necessary to ask, just before his death on the verge of a tonal and colouristic conversion, induced by the bright light and colour of the East? Attractive as the idea may be, I believe the answer is, no. Wilkie was committed to his dark gospel of brown, and had he lived to finish his oriental oil compositions or his pristine, glowing *Knox Sacrament,* no doubt they would have been totally altered and muffled in character by the application of deep toning glazes. Furthermore, we can hardly doubt that Wilkie would have been shocked by the appearance of a Holman Hunt, and it is a fine stroke of irony that his technical influence on a member of the younger generation should have been to encourage extremes of tone, and colouristic tendencies of a sort that he spent at least half of his working life in endeavouring to combat.

1. Letter from Wilkie to Perry Nursey, dated 30 January 1818, British Library, Department of Manuscripts, MS Additional 29,991.

2. *Cunningham,* vol.1, p.482.

3. *Cunningham,* vol.2, pp.73-74 and W. Wilkie Collins, *Memoirs of the life of William Collins* 2 vols, London 1848, vol.1, pp.198-99.

4. G. F. Waagen, *Works of art and artists in England* 3 vols, London 1838, vol.2, pp.292-93.

5. Sarah Uwins, *A Memoir of Thomas Uwins* 2 vols, London 1858, vol.2, pp.259-60.

6. Letter from Wilkie to Perry Nursey dated 30 December 1818, British Library, Department of Manuscripts, MS Additional 29,991.

7. Letter from Wilkie to Sir William Knighton dated 5 January 1831, Mitchell Library, Glasgow.

8. John Burnet, *Recollections of my contemporaries, The early days of Wilkie* in *The Art Journal* 1860, p.237. This account is by far the most convincing version of the episode which seems to have prompted Walter Thornbury's garbled account of how Wilkie 'on a hanging-day, maliciously suspended a Rembrandt among the modern pictures . . . to deride the Turnerians'—an action quite out of keeping with Wilkie's character.

9. Both in the Tate Gallery. The *Pilate* was exhibited in 1830. Butlin and Joll in *The Paintings of J. M. W. Turner* 2 vols, Newhaven and London 1977, suggest a date of c.1832 for the *Christ,* and repeat Davies' suggestion that Turner's architecture is 'Romish', and the picture itself an Anti-Catholic one—a further connection with Wilkie's *Knox.*

10. Letter from Wilkie to Perry Nursey dated 20 November 1822, British Library, Department of Manuscripts, MS Additional 29,991.

11. Letter from Wilkie to Perry Nursey dated 26 July 1823, British Library, Department of Manuscripts, MS Additional 29,991.

12. John Burnet, *The progress of a painter in the nineteenth century* London 1854, p.136.

13. In the Scottish National Portrait Gallery.

14. National Library of Scotland, Department of Manuscripts, MS 9994, f.166.

15. *Cunningham,* vol.1, p.460.

16. National Library of Scotland, Department of Manuscripts, MS 9836, f.52.

17. Letter to Perry Nursey, dated 27 February 1823, British Library, Department of Manuscripts, MS Additional 29,991.

18. David and Francina Irwin, *Scottish Painters at home and abroad,* London 1975, p.195. The painting itself is included in the Scottish National Portrait Gallery's exhibition catalogue, *Treasures of Fyvie* 4 July-29 September 1985, no.59.

19. Letter to Sir William Knighton, dated 14 January 1839, Mitchell Library, Glasgow.

20. Letter to Sir William Knighton, dated 11 June 1838, Mitchell Library, Glasgow.

21. Letter dated 31 March 1840, British Library, Department of Manuscripts, MS Additional 40608.

22. I am grateful to Sara Stevenson for drawing my attention to Alexander Hill's obituary in *The Scotsman* for 16 June 1866.

23. A drawing by D. O. Hill, RSA 1482, in the Prints and Drawings Department, NGS, transferred from the RSA.

24. Marcia Pointon, *William Dyce* Oxford 1979, p.198.

25. Sarah Uwins, *A Memoir of Thomas Uwins* 2 vols, London 1858, vol.1, pp.242-44.

26. *The maid of Saragossa,* Royal Collection. Her exploit had already been celebrated visually, by Goya, and poetically, by Byron.

27. Letter from Wilkie to Sir William Knighton, dated from Limerick, 30 August 1835, Mitchell Library, Glasgow.

28. MS transcript of a letter to Sir Robert Peel, dated from Jerusalem, 18 March 1841, British Library, Department of Manuscripts, MS Additional 40608. This transcript differs in one or two small points throughout the letter from that given in *Cunningham,* vol.3, pp.414-19.

29. Holman Hunt, *Pre-Raphaelitism and the Pre-Raphaelite Brotherhood* 2 vols, London 1905, vol.1, p.53.

30. John Burnet, *The progress of a painter in the nineteenth century* London 1854, p.22.

Transmission of Wilkie's Pictures by Engraving

IN an American children's novel of the mid-1850s[1] a group of young people are described as arranging tableaux vivants for the entertainment of adult visitors. These 'living pictures' for which the children dressed and posed, were based on engravings of famous works of art chosen out of a large portfolio. Reynolds' *Fortitude* and Retzch's *Chess Players* were amongst those selected. Also included was a scene of Alfred in the neatherd's hut where a servant with a comical face was blowing on the burnt cakes to cool them. This amusing subject, unattributed in the novel, is quite clearly, from the description, nothing less than Wilkie's *Alfred* of 1806, a painting which none of the young actors involved in creating the tableaux could ever have seen in the original.

In another part of the world, equally remote from the scene of Wilkie's own activity, a Russian artist, Pavel Andreyevich Fedotov, painted c.1850 his *Poor Aristocrat's Breakfast,* closely and deliberately modelled upon Wilkie's *Letter of Introduction.* Fedotov had not visited England, nor had *The Letter* travelled to Russia, but the engraving of *The Letter* by Burnet must have performed the journey.[2]

In this century, with all our technology for photographing and reproducing works of art we are too apt to regard engravings as inaccurate, colourless, mechanical and boring, and to overlook what these two anecdotes vouch for, their creative vitality.

By far the larger part of the nineteenth-century British population to whom Wilkie as an artist was a household name had never seen any of his

71. Pavel Andreyevich Fedotov
A poor aristocrat's breakfast

paintings. Nevertheless, mentions by Hazlitt or Walter Scott of *The Blind Fiddler*.[3] Wilson's allusion to *The Village Politicians* in the *Noctes*,[4] or Jerrold's ingenious re-creation of *The Rent Day* and *Distraining* in a stage drama,[5] were immediately understood. Wilkie's actual paintings were shown for a brief period at the R.A. and then disappeared into collections—which were usually private ones. Occasionally they were re-exhibited, and sometimes they passed through the salerooms or were seen by favoured young artists visiting Sheepshanks or Wells of Redleaf, but what the general reader recognised in Hazlitt, Scott, Wilson or Jerrold was a line engraving hanging on his own, or some friend's wall, or glimpsed for sale in a print shop window. It was not necessary to possess the engraving in order to be familiar with its appearance. Henry Merritt, writing in 1872, says of Wilkie, 'For many years the windows of the chief print-shops were monopolised by fine line engravings after his works, and [they] are thus familiar to all but the rising generation. Of late years we have missed the "Greenwich Pensioners" [a mistake for "Chelsea Pensioners"], "The Rent Day", "The Penny Wedding", "Blind Man's Buff", "Distraining for Rent" and many other subjects which in their day served to detain and to amuse, not to say instruct and improve, the passengers in our great thoroughfares.'[6]

The benefits of engravings for the painter were twofold. In the first place, as Leslie pointed out, they financed the artist's original works. 'Even Wilkie would not have been what he was but for this art. The prices he received for his finest pictures, at the time when he painted but one a year, would never have enabled him to give them their admirable finish, but for the remuneration he received from his prints.'[7] It is, however, the second benefit, the transmission of the painter's imagery and the expansion of his reputation via prints which we are mainly concerned with here. The engraving by Burnet of *The Blind Fiddler* was organised and published by Boydell. Wilkie received a mere fifty pounds for this—the same price that he had initially received for the picture itself—and was told by several well-wishers that this was far too little. Sir George Beaumont suggested that it would have been better for Wilkie himself to have opened a subscription for the engraving after his painting,[8] and this subsequently was what he did with later subjects. Burnet's print proved a great success, though his behaviour whilst he was in sole charge of the painting of *The Blind Fiddler* caused Wilkie a good deal of anxiety,[9] nor was Wilkie happy with the first proofs and compelled Burnet to make substantial changes. Further disagreements took place over the financial arrangements for a companion print, which Burnet found unsatisfactory. In 1812 Wilkie therefore proposed to the engraver Raimbach whom he had known for five years, a joint-stock adventure in which the painter would enjoy a quarter share in any profits.[10] The first picture selected was *The Village Politicians*, published 1 January 1814, and subsequent ventures included *The Rent Day, Blind Man's Buff* and *Distraining for Rent*. Such an arrangement not only brought Wilkie a greater financial reward, but enabled him to keep an eye on the whole engraving process from beginning to end, so that he could offer suggestions or make retouches where necessary. During his career Wilkie was involved with many engravers besides Raimbach— Burnet, James Stewart and Doo all engraved important paintings, but the general process seems to have been much the same in every case. Since the painting to be engraved had generally already been sold by the artist it was necessary to persuade the buyer to part with his treasure for an indefinite period of between one to three years. To maintain quality the engraver required the presence of the actual painting. In the case of *The Village Politicians* Raimback kept it for sixteen months. The contact with

72. Burnet's engraving of the small boy in *The blind fiddler* (detail)
effectively conveys Wilkie's painterly style in 1806

the publisher Moon for Doo's engraving of *Knox preaching* stipulated that
the engraver should have it on loan for three years, but in fact the engraving took several months longer than this and Sir Robert Peel the owner
began to grow very restive.[11] The Knox was insured against fire whilst it
was with the engraver and its edges were protected by a temporary wood
slip frame, but the painting was obviously always at some risk of damage
during this period. Burnet greatly annoyed Wilkie by removing *The Blind
Fiddler* to some unknown hiding hole without either asking permission of
the owner, Sir George Beaumont, or providing Wilkie with the opportunity
of checking its safety.[12]

The first stage in the engraving process was the so-called 'etching' by
which the main outlines of the figures and setting were transferred to the
copper. This process did not take very long, and the etched lines, being on
the faint side, were swallowed up and vanished when the plate had been
completed. There were two possible methods of engraving, line or mezzotint, and Wilkie favoured the former. The seemingly rather limited
vocabulary of lines, straight or wavy, even or varying in width, shallow or
deep (the deeper the line, the blacker the print) single or crossing each
other, long or short, combined with the occasional dot, was surprisingly
well able to cope with reproducing the full tonal and textural range of a
complex oil painting. At a certain distance these lines cease to be read as
such and appear as gradated tones instead. 'A line engraver,' Burnet
remarked, 'expresses the luminous and prominent parts by a series of short
dots, as if the lines were crossed by touches of white chalk, while in the

73. Burnet's engraving of a detail in *The reading of a will* shows how Wilkie's style had changed in the fourteen years that separate the two paintings

shades and retiring portions his lines are smooth and undisturbed.'[13] The subscribers to the engraving received the best quality proof prints, which were also the most expensive; ordinary prints on sale to the general public were about half the price of the proofs. The proofs of *The Village Politicians* cost four guineas each, the ordinary impressions two. Obviously there was a wider circulation at more social levels of prints costing two guineas than of original paintings costing thirty to several hundred but equally obviously all talk of engravings bringing art into the labourer's cottage was merely a figure of speech. No labourer on the wages of the day could possibly have spent two guineas on a print. The numbers of impressions issued are of some interest. The proofs of course were limited editions. The five hundred proofs of *Blind Man's Buff* were found to be excessive and half this number turned out to be about right. Ordinary impressions continued to be printed and sold for decades after they were first issued. By 1842 the sales of prints after *The Rent Day* had reached to between four and five thousand. Such figures were not achieved without much wear on the plates. These being copper, which is a soft metal, soon lost their pristine sharpness and required not only constant small repairs but even occasional complete re-engraving. Despite this they were regarded as a good enough investment for buyers to offer two and three hundred pounds apiece for the old plates of subjects such as *Blind Man's Buff, The Rent Day* and *Village Politicians* in the Wilkie auction sale of 1841. New prints from certain of

Wilkie's plates are still being issued to this day but their quality is by now rather defective.

Who owned these prints? One answer is provided via collectors' sale catalogues. The catalogues for instance of the private collections of those Scottish artists most influenced by Wilkie, witness to the importance of the engravings. William Allan owned a proof print of *The Rabbit on the Wall,* and no less than three prints, two of them proofs, of *The Letter of Introduction.* Thomas Duncan owned Burnet's engraving of *The Reading of the Will* and a presentation proof of *Columbus.* John Phillip, who possessed an oil sketch for *The Village Politicians* and a pen study for *The Chelsea Pensioners* also owned Burnet's engravings of *The Blind Fiddler* and *The Reading of the Will* and Stewart's *Penny Wedding.* Further investigation would yield much more information, but it is evident even from this that the owner or painter of fine originals had no objection to owning prints as well.

Having established the importance and wide dissemination of the prints, it becomes necessary to ask what aspects exactly of Wilkie's paintings the engraver was able to transmit and what he had to leave out. Here one must be very careful. One is rashly inclined to suppose that a photograph, especially a coloured one, tells everything about a painting, because it is a mechanical replica, forgetting that it only reproduces stains or patches of light, dark and colour. Paintings are three-dimensional objects however—some more so than others—and the thickness and texture or weight of the paint, which the photographer can only indicate by angling his lights to relieve the ridges and bumps with shadow can be represented by the sensitive engraver through variations in the character of his lines. Between *The Blind Fiddler* and *Reading the Will* Wilkie's personal style changed considerably, and Burnett's two engravings do more than simply record the contents of the two pictures, they also express the style of each—the flat, edgy rather slippery quality of *The Fiddler* and the softer, rounded and more exquisite and painterly *Will.* Similarly the exquisite delicacy and refinement of the painting in *Blind Man's Buff* is most convincingly conveyed by Raimbach. The engraver was not a mechanic but himself a creative artist. Wilkie described Doo's engraving of the *Knox preaching* as 'this translation or version of it (for its merits are far above a copy) into a new language'.[14] His choice of phrase was echoed by Burnet, 'We must always bear in mind that an engraving is not a copy of a picture,—it is a translation'.[15] His engravers, men like Raimbach and Burnet, were highly intelligent, with creative mentalities and well developed critical faculties. Burnet in particular was an art critic and theorist as well as a painter. Having trained alongside Wilkie as a student in Edinburgh he understood much of what Wilkie was trying to do, and because he understood was able to find a successful interpretation. Nevertheless, the engraving was bound to be more effective in presenting Wilkie as a narrator or inventor of situations and characters than Wilkie the manipulator of pigments and glazes. Since Wilkie's narrations and situations nearly all turn on character and behaviour we need to examine exactly what happens to this under the engraver's tool. Most of his paintings were fairly small, and the engravings were rather large, so there is no great loss of size. If, however, one examines Wilkie's own chalk study for the boy's head in *The Letter,* his painting of the same head, and Burnet's engraving of it, one perceives in the painting a very high degree of subtlety in the expression gained by compressing or reducing the large chalk study to correct dimensions for the painted panel. There is in Burnet's engraving, a further small reduction in size but a startling loss of subtlety. The expression has coarsened, the face hardened. Possibilities conveyed by Wilkie are shut out by Burnet. Since the engraver works with line on metal he must select and reject where the painter can slur definite boundaries. Much the same thing happens to the small boy's face in *The Blind Fiddler.* It has been hardened by the engraving to a comic, almost grotesquely comic mask, and aged too, losing the full sense of spontaneous impromptu mischief Wilkie gave it. One of the points of disagreement between Wilkie and Burnet was the head and hat of this child as it was first engraved. Yet when all this has been said, the engravings cannot be dismissed. Treating Wilkie's young man or mischievous small boy as if they were real people, we can see that they still outlive their transmigration from paint to copper as the same recognisable entities. Their basic personalities somehow or other continue, and so too do those of *The Blind Fiddler, Duncan Gray* and scores of others—the same but simplified. Two art lovers analysing the character of *The Blind Fiddler,* one knowing only the painting, the other only the print, would certainly be able to follow each other's arguments.

The prints we have been discussing up till now were high quality engravings of ample size, authorised by the painter himself and worked with the original painting in view as a model. Not all Wilkie prints in circulation were like this. Many others were small. Some were even tiny. Pirated prints were produced and were in circulation both in this country and abroad, where the French were familiar with *Le lapin sur le Mur* and *Le Colin Maillard,* illicit versions of *The Rabbit on the Wall* and *Blind Man's Buff.*[16] Prints which consisted of mere outlines without a vestige of tone or shading also existed giving an oddly neo-classical touch to *The Rent Day* and *Blind Man's Buff.*[17] The regrettable thing about all such specimens is not so much their small size as the fact that they were engraved from engravings not from the original paintings—copies of copies in fact. Proofs of this can be found in two small and nearly identical prints after the second version of Wilkie's *Duncan Gray,* one engraved by T. Ranson in 1822, and the other by Greatbach for *The Wilkie Gallery.* This *Duncan Gray* belonged to George Thomson and differed quite distinctly from its prototype *The Refusal,* belonging to Sheepshanks. Ranson's engraving correctly records the owner and publisher as George Thomson. Greatbach gives Sheepshanks as the owner, a mistake which would have been incredible if he had really borrowed the actual painting from Thomson, or

74. Wilkie's rendering of the complex expression on the boy's face
in *The letter of introduction* (*cat.21* detail)

75. Burnet's engraving of the boy's head in *The letter of introduction*
(detail) lacks the subtlety of Wilkie's original

Thomson's successor. *The Wilkie Gallery,* a collection of prints after Wilkie, issued, together with letterpress by Henry Bartlett about 1849–50, is normally found now bound up as a single or as a pair of large volumes, and the frequency of its occurrence suggests that it did more than any of the other sets of engravings to disseminate first knowledge of Wilkie's art and ultimately perhaps disparagement of and contempt for it. Some of these Wilkie Gallery engravings may have been worked directly from the originals. In many other instances this seems unlikely or impossible. The quality is at times very moderate and the subtleties of facial expression and posture are almost entirely eliminated in works like *The Letter of Introduction* or *Reading of the Will.* The ultimate degradation of Wilkie's work is, however, reached in a set of coloured prints issued as a supplement by the *Glasgow Weekly Herald* in 1892. It is a little difficult to determine the exact technical process used on these. The old copper engravings had to be re-inked by hand for each printing, and the printing itself was done under strong pressure. Intaglio engravings cannot be printed at the same time as raised typefaces. The *Herald* prints on the other hand were obviously run off in huge numbers by the same process and at the same time as the letterpress. They were probably copied— perhaps by some photographic method—from existing engravings. These last had certainly been coloured, in a bizarre attempt to provide them with some eye appeal, by hand, and it is this hand colouring, not the colouring of Wilkie, which has been reproduced. The colourist had probably never seen the originals and merely followed his or her own fancy. In *Distraining* for example, most of the coat and waistcoat colours are completely wrong. Only occasionally, by chance, the colourist has hit on the right tint. Yet the *Glasgow Weekly Herald* must have supposed these would be popular. Stripped of painterly style, refined draughtsmanship, expression of character, even their true colour, as these prints have been, one wonders what the publishers believed they were offering. All that is left when everything else has been removed are some small fuzzily drawn and crudely coloured figures arranged in striking groupings, mnemonic images that seem to belong on a biscuit tin lid or printed tea tray, yet attesting simply by virtue of their reduction to such cheap and pointless absurdity, to the most absolute and touching faith in their power as works of art to survive and redeem every possible disfigurement and disgrace. It is, really, a triumph of a sort for Wilkie's art.

1. Elizabeth Wetherell, *Melbourne House.*

2. Fedotov is known to have studied prints after Wilkie and Hogarth, but it has not proved possible to discover which prints he had seen.

3. See p.52, notes 15 and 16.

4. See p.69, note 6.

5. See p.62.

6. *Henry Merrit, Pictures in the International Exhibition* (of 1872), reprinted in Anna Lea Merrit, *Henry Merrit, Art Criticism and Romance* 2 vols, 1879, vol.1, p.190.

7. *Autobiographical recollections of Charles Robert Leslie* ed. Tom Taylor, 2 vols, London 1860, vol.1, p.215.

8. *The Diary of Joseph Farington* ed. Kathryn Cave, vol.10, Newhaven and London 1982, entry for 7 May 1810, p.3649.

9. *Memoirs and recollections of the late Abraham Raimbach, Esq. Engraver, including a memoir of Sir David Wilkie* ed. M. T. S. Raimbach, London 1843.

10. Letter from Wilkie to Sir Robert Peel dated 29 November 1837, British Library, Department of Manuscripts, MS Additional 40607, f.242-243.

11. John Burnet, *Comparative merits of line engraving and mezzotint in Practical Essays on various branches of the fine arts* London 1848, p.147.

12. Letter from Wilkie to Peel, op. cit. (note 10).

13. John Burnet, op. cit. (note 11), p.133.

14. I am grateful to Dr Marcia Pointon for lending me the manuscript of her article on French engravings after Wilkie, *From Blind Man's Buff to Le Colin Maillard : Wilkie and his French audience.*

ABBREVIATIONS USED IN CATALOGUE

B.I. = British Institution

N.G.S. = National Gallery of Scotland

R.A. = Royal Academy of Arts

R.I. = Royal Institution for the encouragement of the fine arts, Scotland

R.S.A. = Royal Scottish Academy of Arts

S.N.P.G. = Scottish National Portrait Gallery

Cunningham = Allan Cunningham, *The life of Sir David Wilkie,* 3 vols. London 1843

Catalogue of Exhibits

All measurements are in centimetres, height preceding width.

Major exhibition dates until the 1850s are provided as
an indication of the occasions on which works in private collections
would have been available for public viewing by artists.

FOLKLORE AND THE VERNACULAR TRADITION

WILKIE
1. *Self-portrait*
Painted c.1804–5.
Oil on canvas 74.3 × 61
Scottish National Portrait Gallery

WILKIE
2. *Pitlessie Fair*
Signed: *D.Wilkie/Pinxt. 1804*. Shows the annual
agricultural fair held in May at Pitlessie in the
Parish of Cults where the painter's father was
Minister. Painted for Charles Kinnear of Kin-
loch. See pp.6–13.
Oil on canvas 58.5 × 106.7
Exh: Pall Mall, London 1812; R.I. Edinburgh 1821;
R.S.A. 1844
National Gallery of Scotland

WILKIE
3. *The Penny Wedding*
Signed and dated: *David Wilkie 1818*. Shows a
traditional Scottish country wedding celebration
at which monetary contributions were made by
the guests. See pp.18–23.
Oil on panel 64.4 × 95.6
Exh: R.A. 1819; R.S.A. 1829; B.I. 1842 and 1850
Engraved by James Stewart 1832
Lent by Her Majesty The Queen

WILKIE
4. *The death of the red deer*
Signed and dated: *D. Wilkie 1821*. Painted by
Wilkie after a visit to the Duke of Atholl in 1817.
This shows McIntyre and McGregor, The Duke of
Atholl's stalker, and piper. The Duke was a cele-
brated sportsman. See p.23.
Oil on panel 24.1 × 34.2
Engraved by P. Lightfoot
Exh: B.I. 1821 and 1842
Lent by His Grace the Duke of Atholl from Blair Castle

GEIKIE, Walter (Scottish) 1795–1837
5. *The fruit-seller*
Signed and dated: *Wr. Geikie 1824*.
Oil on panel 40.6 × 34.3
National Gallery of Scotland

GEIKIE
6. *Scottish roadside scene*
Signed: *Wr. Geikie*.
Oil on canvas 40.6 × 61
National Gallery of Scotland

HOWE, James (Scottish) 1780–1836
7. *Skirling Fair (Stallions)*
Oil on canvas 81.2 × 120.6
Lent anonymously

SHEILS, William (Scottish) 1785–1857
8. *Return from Market*
Signed: *W SHIELS RSA EDIN*.
Oil on canvas 70.2 × 118
Lent anonymously

PHILLIP, John (Scottish) 1817–1867
9. *A Scotch Fair*
Dated: 1848. See pp.13–14.
Oil on canvas 92 × 137.5
Lent by Aberdeen Art Gallery and Museum

HARVEY, Sir George (Scottish) 1806–76
10. *The Curlers*
A study for the large finished picture exhibited at
the R.S.A. in 1835. See p.13.
Oil on canvas 35.9 × 79.4
National Gallery of Scotland

LANDSEER, Sir Edwin (English) 1802–73
11. The Duke of Atholl's Keeper John Crerar, with his pony
Painted at Blair Atholl in 1824 as a sketch in connection with Landseer's preparatory work on *The death of the stag in Glen Tilt*. See p.24.
Oil on board 58.4 × 43.0
Lent by Perth Museum and Art Gallery

LANDSEER
12. Highland interior
Painted c.1830.
Oil on panel 69.8 × 85
Lent anonymously

SIMSON, William (Scottish) 1800–47
13. Twelfth of August
A sketch for a larger picture painted 1829.
Oil on panel 24.1 × 39.4
National Gallery of Scotland

SIMSON
14. A goatherd's cottage
Signed and dated: *Wm. Simson 1832.*
Oil on panel 49.2 × 67.3
National Gallery of Scotland

FRASER, Alexander (Scottish) 1786–1865
15. A Highland sportsman
Signed and dated: *Alex. Fraser/1832.*
Oil on panel 78.1 × 109.3
National Gallery of Scotland

CARSE, Alexander (Scottish) active from 1780–d.1843
16. The Penny Wedding
Possibly 1819.
Oil on canvas 88.2 × 131.5
Lent by Flight Lieutenant G. N. Statham

PHILLIP, John (Scottish) 1817–67
17. Presbyterian Catechising
Signed and dated: *John Phillip 1847*
Oil on canvas 100.6 × 156
National Gallery of Scotland

ORCHARDSON, Sir William Quiller (Scottish) 1832–1910
18. The Queen of the Swords
Signed: *W. Q. Orchardson.* Shows a sword dance on Shetland, as described by Scott in *The Pirate.* Study for a picture of 1877. See p.24.
Oil on canvas 47.3 × 80.6
National Gallery of Scotland

CHARACTER AND NARRATIVE

WILKIE
19. The blind fiddler
Signed and dated: *D. Wilkie 1806.* Shows an itinerant fiddler who, with his wife, child and baby, has stopped to entertain the family of a cobbler. See pp.32–36.
Oil on panel 57.8 × 79.4
Exh: R.A. 1807; B.I. 1825
Engraved by John Burnet, and by C. W. Sharpe for *The Wilkie Gallery*
Lent by the Trustees of the Tate Gallery

WILKIE
20. Village Politicians. Vide Scotland's Skaith
Signed and dated: *D. Wilkie 1806.*
Scotland's Skaith is a poem by Hector MacNeill describing the downfall of a family through the father's addictions to political discussion and whisky. This was painted by Wilkie in London for Lord Mansfield, but was modelled on an earlier version of the subject painted in Scotland. See pp.28–31, 54–59.
Oil on canvas 57.2 × 75
Exh: R.A. 1806
Engraved by Raimbach, and by C. W. Sharpe for *The Wilkie Gallery*
Lent by the Rt Hon. the Earl of Mansfield

WILKIE
21. The Letter of Introduction
Signed and dated: *D. Wilkie 1813.* Shows a young man who has brought a letter of introduction to a suspicious elderly connoisseur. Based on an incident in Wilkie's own life when he first came to London. See pp.40–43.
Oil on panel 61 × 50.2
Exh: R.A. 1814
Engraved by Burnet, and by Greatbach for *The Wilkie Gallery*
National Gallery of Scotland

WILKIE
22. Duncan Gray
An illustration to Burns' poem *Duncan Gray.* Duncan woos Maggie and is refused, despite her parents' intercession. Just as, in a temper, he decides to abandon his courtship she relents. An earlier, slightly larger version of the subject was painted by Wilkie in 1814 (now Victoria and Albert Museum). See pp.16–17.
Oil on panel 36.8 × 32
Exh: (probably) R.I., Edinburgh 1824
Engraved by T. Ranson, and by Greatbach for *The Wilkie Gallery*
National Gallery of Scotland

BIRD, Edward (English) 1772–1819

23. *The Country Choristers*

Signed and dated: *E. Bird/1810*. Shows village choir rehearsing an anthem for Sunday. See p.36.
Oil on panel 62.9 × 92.7
Lent by Her Majesty the Queen

TURNER, Joseph Mallord William (English) 1775–1851

24. *The Cobbler's home*

Painted c.1825. See p.37.
Oil on panel 59.7 × 80.0
Lent by the Trustees of the Tate Gallery

LIZARS, William Home (Scottish) 1788–1859

25. *Reading the will*

First exhibited Associated Artists Edinburgh 1811. See p.37.
Panel 51.5 × 64.8
National Gallery of Scotland

BURNET, John (Scottish) 1784–1868

26. *An oyster-cellar in Leith*

Painted c.1819.
Oil on panel 29.2 × 35.5
National Gallery of Scotland

FAED, Thomas (Scottish) 1826–1900

27. *The poor, the poor man's friend*

Signed and dated: *Thomas Faed 1867*. Shows an elderly blind beggar approaching a fisherman's cottage. See p.64.
Canvas 40.6 × 61
Lent by the Victoria and Albert Museum

HAYDON, Benjamin Robert (English) 1786–1846

28. *Waiting for the Times*

Painted 1831. See pp.56–57.
Oil on canvas 64 × 75
Lent by Times Newspapers Limited

KIDD, William (Scottish) 1769–1863

29. *Asleep*

Signed: *W. Kidd*.
Oil on panel 43.4 × 32.3
Lent by the Patrick Allan Fraser of Hospitalfield Trust

KIDD

30. *Self-portrait of the artist with his wife*

Oil on panel 42.5 × 33
Lent by the Patrick Allan Fraser of Hospitalfield Trust

MULREADY, William (Irish) 1786–1863

31. *The village buffoon*

Painted 1816. See p.46.
Oil on canvas 73.7 × 62.2
Lent by the Royal Academy of Arts

MULREADY

32. *The Widow*

Signed and dated: *Wm Mulready 1823*. See p.46.
Oil on canvas laid on panel 68.5 × 80
Lent by William Proby, Esq., Elton Hall

COPE, Charles West (English) 1811–90

33. *Palpitation*

Signed and dated: *C. W. Cope 1844*. See p.47.
Panel 76.2 × 57.8
Lent by the Victoria and Albert Museum

STEPHANOFF, Francis Phillip (English) 1790–1860

34. *Answering an advertisement—Wanted a respectable female, as housekeeper to a middle aged gentleman of serious and domestic habits*

Signed: *F. P. Stephanoff*. First exhibited R.A. 1841. See p.43.
Oil on canvas 62.2 × 74.9
Lent by Glasgow Art Gallery and Museum

REDGRAVE, Richard (English) 1804–88

35. *Fashion's slaves*

First exhibited R.A. 1847. See pp.43–44.
Oil on panel 61 × 75
Lent anonymously

CAMPBELL, James (English) 1828–93

36. *Waiting for legal advice*

Signed and dated: *J. Campbell Junior/1857*. A scene in a solicitor's office. See pp.44–45.
Oil on board 77.5 × 63.5
Lent by the Walker Art Gallery, Liverpool

MODERN LIFE

WILKIE

37. *Distraining for rent*

signed and dated: *D. Wilkie 1815*. Shows the bailiff and two assistants listing the possessions of a farmer who has failed to pay his rent. His property will be sold and he himself with his family, evicted. See pp.50–51, 59–63.
Oil on panel 81.3 × 123
Exh: R.A. 1815; B.I. 1816 and 1842; R.S.A. 1846
Engraved by Raimbach, and by W. Greatbach for *The Wilkie Gallery*
National Gallery of Scotland

WILKIE

38. *Chelsea Pensioners receiving the London Gazette Extraordinary of Thursday, June 22d, 1815, announcing the Battle of Waterloo!!!*

Signed and dated: *David Wilkie 1822*. Commissioned by the Duke of Wellington in 1816. See pp.64–66.
Oil on panel 97 × 158
Exh: R.A. 1822; B.I. 1825; R.S.A. 1837; B.I. 1842
Engraved by Burnet, and by Greatbach for *The Wilkie Gallery*
Lent by the Trustees of the Victoria and Albert Museum, Apsley House

COLLINSON, James (English) 1825–81

39. *Answering the Emigrant's letter*

> Signed and dated: *J. Collinson 1850*. See p.63.
> Oil on panel 70.1 × 91.2
> Lent by City of Manchester Art Galleries

REDGRAVE, Richard (English) 1804–88

40. *The Outcast*

> Signed and dated: *Rich. Redgrave 1851*. See p.64.
> Oil on canvas 78.7 × 104.2
> Lent by the Royal Academy of Arts

FAED, Thomas (Scottish) 1826–1900

41. *Forgiven*

> Signed: *Thomas Faed*. A study for the finished
> picture of 1874. See p.64.
> Oil on canvas 35.5 × 48.2
> Lent by Guildhall Art Gallery, Corporation of London

FAED

42. *From dawn to sunset*

> Signed: *Faed*. First exhibited R.A. 1861.
> See p.64.
> Oil on canvas 84 × 109
> Lent anonymously

MARTINEAU, Robert Braithwaite (English)
1826–69

43. *Last day in the Old Home*

> Signed and dated: *Robt. B. Martineau 1862*.
> See p.64.
> Oil on canvas 107.3 × 144.7
> Lent by the Trustees of the Tate Gallery

MULREADY, William (Irish) 1786–1863

44. *The Convalescent from Waterloo*

> Commenced 1822. See p.68.
> Oil on panel 61 × 77.5
> Lent by the Victoria and Albert Museum

FRITH, William Powell (English) 1819–1909

45. *The railway station*

> Signed and dated: *W. P. Frith fect 1862*. A view of
> Paddington Station. See p.67.
> Oil on canvas 116.7 × 256.4
> Lent by the Royal Holloway College
> (University of London)

RELIGION, HISTORY AND TRAVEL

WILKIE

46. *The preaching of John Knox before the Lords of Congregation, 10th June 1559*

> Signed and dated: *D. Wilkie f 1832*. A reduced
> replica by the artist of the large painting of 1832
> (Tate Gallery). Shows Knox preaching at St
> Andrews to hostile Catholic Bishops and to sup-
> porters of the reformed religion. See pp.70–73.
> Oil on canvas 45.7 × 54
> National Gallery of Scotland

WILKIE

47. *The Irish whiskey still*

> Signed and dated: *David Wilkie f. 1840*. Painted
> after the artist's visit to Ireland in 1835. See p.83.
> Oil on panel 119.4 × 158
> National Gallery of Scotland

WILKIE

48. *Cardinals, Priests and Roman Citizens washing the Pilgrims' feet*

> Signed and dated: *David Wilkie, Roma, 1827*.
> Shows a ceremony that took place during Holy
> Week in the Convent of the Santa Trinita dei
> Pellegrini. See p.81.
> Oil on canvas 49.5 × 73.7
> Exh: R.A. 1829
> Lent by Glasgow Art Gallery and Museum

WILKIE

49. *John Knox dispensing the Sacrament at Calder House*

> An unfinished sketch for the large picture
> (*cat.50*). See pp.77–79.
> Oil on panel 45.1 × 61
> Engraved by J. Telford in the *Art Union*
> National Gallery of Scotland

WILKIE

50. *John Knox dispensing the Sacrament at Calder House*

> Unfinished picture painted to be engraved as a
> companion to *Knox Preaching*. Shows one of the
> earliest celebrations of the Protestant Sacra-
> ment in the home of the Sandilands, adherents to
> the reformed religion. See pp.78, 92–93.
> Oil on panel 123.2 × 165
> Exh: R.S.A. 1843
> National Gallery of Scotland

WILKIE

51. *A Persian prince, his slave bringing him sherbet*

> Signed and dated: *D. Wilkie f. Constantinople
> Octbr 1840*. Wilkie planned to use the features of
> the sitter, Halicoo Mirza, whom he described as 'a
> great Persian Prince' for the face of Christ in his
> projected gospel subjects.

Chalk and colour wash, heightened with body colour on buff paper 45.7 × 31.5
Lithographed by J. Nash for volume 2 of *Sir David Wilkie's Sketches in Spain, Italy and the East* 1847.
Lent by Aberdeen Art Gallery and Museums

WILKIE
52. *The Turkish letter writer*
Signed and dated: *D. Wilkie f. Constantinople 1840.*
Oil on panel 71.7 × 54
Exh: B.I. 1842
Engraved by R. Staines for *The Wilkie Gallery*
Lent by Aberdeen Art Gallery and Museums

WILKIE
53. *An Arab Muleteer*
Shows the muleteer who accompanied Wilkie from Jerusalem to Jaffa in April 1841. He is depicted at prayer. See p.88.
Black and red chalk with coloured wash 54.6 × 38.3
Lithographed by J. Nash for volume 2 of *Sir David Wilkie's Sketches in Spain, Italy and the East* 1847.
National Gallery of Scotland

HARVEY, Sir George (Scottish) 1806–76
54. *The Covenanters' preaching*
First exhibited R.S.A. 1830. See p.75.
Oil on panel 82.6 × 106.7
Lent by Glasgow Art Gallery and Museum

ALLAN, Sir William (Scottish) 1782–1850
55. *Murder of David Rizzio*
Signed: *W. Allan.* First exhibited R.A. 1833. See pp.73–75.
Oil on panel 102.9 × 163
National Gallery of Scotland

WINDUS, William Lindsay (English) 1822–1907
56. *Morton before Claverhouse at Tillietudlem*
A sketch for the larger picture of 1847. Illustrates a scene from Scott's *Old Mortality.* See p.76.
Oil on board 23 × 29
Lent by the Walker Art Gallery, Liverpool

DOUGLAS, Sir William Fettes (Scottish) 1822–91
57. *Wishart preaching against Mariolatry*
First exhibited R.S.A. 1871.
Oil on canvas 78.1 × 175
National Gallery of Scotland

DYCE, William (Scottish) 1806–64
58. *John Knox dispensing the Sacrament at Calder House*
See pp.78–79
Oil on canvas 38.8 × 59.6
Lent by John Knox House, Edinburgh

DRUMMOND, James (Scottish) 1816–77
59. *George Wishart on his way to execution administering the Scarament for the first time in Protestant form*
Signed in monogram and dated: *JD 1845.*
See p.78.
Oil on canvas 76.8 × 106.7
Lent by Dundee Art Galleries and Museums

LAUDER, Robert Scott (Scottish) 1803–69
60. *Study for Christ teacheth humility*
A study for the large picture of 1847. See p.89.
Oil on canvas 31.1 × 56.5
National Gallery of Scotland

NICOL, Erskine (Scottish) 1825–1904
61. *The day after the fair*
First exhibited R.S.A. 1860. See p.83.
Oil on canvas 56 × 81.2
Lent by the Royal Scottish Academy

SIMSON, William (Scottish) 1800–47
62. *A Camaldolese monk showing the relics in the sacristy of a Roman convent*
Signed and dated: *William Simson fect 1838.*
See p.82.
Oil on canvas 129.5 × 104.1
Lent anonymously

LEWIS, John (English) 1805–76
63. *The Arab scribe Cairo*
Signed and dated: *1852.* See p.90.
Watercolour heightened with white 46.5 × 61
Lent anonymously

HUNT, William Holman (English) 1827–1910
64. *Nazareth*
Painted on the spot at Nazareth in 1855. The figures are similarly dressed to the figures of Jesus and the Virgin in Hunt's *Finding of the Saviour in the Temple,* and must be intended to suggest them.
Watercolour heightened with body colour 35.3 × 49.8
Lent by the Whitworth Art Gallery, University of Manchester

ROSSETTI, Dante Gabriel (English) 1828–52
65. *Found* (unfinished)
Painted c.1853 as a study for the unfinished painting of the same subject. See pp.92–93.
Oil on panel 38.1 × 38.1
Lent by Carlisle Museum and Art Gallery

LIST OF ENGRAVINGS AFTER WILKIE'S PAINTINGS

LARGE LINE ENGRAVINGS

1. *Village Politicians*
   engraved by Abraham Raimbach
   published 1 January 1814

2. *The Blind Fiddler*
   engraved by John Burnet
   published 1 October 1811

3. *Rent Day*
   engraved by Abraham Raimbach
   (second plate)

4. *The Letter of Introduction*
   engraved by John Burnet

5. *Duncan Gray*
   engraved by Francis Engleheart
   published 1 February 1828

6. *The Reading of a Will*
   engraved by John Burnet
   published 1 June 1842

ENGRAVINGS FROM *THE WILKIE GALLERY*

7. *Village Politicians*
   engraved by C. W. Sharpe

8. *Duncan Gray*
   engraved by G. Greatbach

9. *The Rabbit on the Wall*
   engraved by W. Greatbach

10. *Reading the Will*
    engraved by W. Greatbach

OTHER ENGRAVINGS

11. *Le Lapin sur le Mur*
    etched and aquatinted by Jazet

12. *Duncan Gray*
    engraved by T. Ranson
    published 1 June 1822

13. *Reading the Will*
    engraved by Bovinet

14. *Duncan Gray*
    engraved by C. Butterworth

15. *The Saviour at Emmaus*
    lithographed by Joseph Nash and
    published 1846 in *Sir David Wilkie's
    sketches in Spain, Italy and the East*,
    volume 2

Six coloured engravings issued as parts
of a series of twelve monthly supplements
to the *Glasgow Weekly Herald,* and
published as a full set of 12 in 1893,
price one shilling.

16. *Village Politicians*
    published 3 September 1892

17. *The Blind Fiddler*
    published 3 May 1892

18. *Distraining for Rent*
    published 7 January 1893

19. *The Penny Wedding*
    published 4 March 1893

20. *Reading the Will*
    published 6 August 1892

21. *The Preaching of John Knox*
    published 1 April 1893

LIST OF ILLUSTRATIONS
An asterisk denotes a picture not included in the exhibition

LIST OF COLOUR PLATES